LET HIM

The believer's journey

LET
HIM

*LIVING LIFE in tune
with GOD*

Vincent H Chough

Cosecha Press

Copyright © 2024 Vincent H Chough
Title: Let Him – Living Life in Tune with God

ISBN: 979-8-9921248-0-4

This book is dedicated to my loving wife, my five beloved sons… and to all those who come to restoration in the risen Lord Jesus Christ.

Contents

IS IT POSSIBLE?

Have you ever experienced those moments when everything flows smoothly in your life? It's that sensation where every move you make falls neatly into place. It might even feel like the external world is working with you to stay on track. Those who read *The Alchemist* would say it's the "universe conspiring" in your favor. Star Wars fans call it "the Force". Others call it "flow". Maybe the feeling lasts for minutes, hours, or even days.

Imagine if you could live your entire life this way. Is it even possible? That's what this book seeks to explore.

You won't find any magical solutions hidden in these pages. This is not a "how to" book, because life isn't so neat and tidy all the time. Instead, we sometimes need to explore stories to help us learn and grow. What you will find here is plenty of honesty and an authentic search for truth – because any kind of flow we might experience in life must be based on truth.

Today's world is full of strife and confusion. The questions and situations that face us have reached epic proportions. It's never been more important to connect with yourself and with your Creator. In these complex and conflict filled times, if we hope to find a sweet spot, a life that flows, a universe conspiring for us, or a force that guides us – it must include God.

At the end of this book, you'll also find supplemental content about cultivating your prayer life. Many have commented on how much it has helped them experience a richer life of prayer.

If you're willing to open your heart and mind,

... if you want to dive deep into a search for truth,

... if you want to be healthy, happy, and free,

... and if you have a sense of exploration and adventure... then this book might just be what you're looking for.

Let's get started.

Chapter 1: Casting out the rats & roaches

It was a scorcher today. This morning, I pulled up to pick up my friend, Ruben. When he opened the car door, a blast of hot humid air rushed in. It's mid-January here in Buenos Aires, Argentina, and we're in the thick of summer in South America.

Ruben squeezed his large frame into my small vehicle, and we sped down the road to his brother Omar's house. Apparently, Omar had fallen ill. He had been sick for a while, but now things were worse. He had heart failure, lung problems, and was severely depressed. Omar also suffered from elephantiasis of the lower limbs. This meant his legs and feet were massively swollen and covered with purple, hard, and thick skin. What could this possibly have to do with flow and living in synchrony with God? Let me explain.

I didn't want to pick up Ruben this morning to drive him to Omar's house. I didn't want to spend all day helping him care for his brother. What I wanted to do was work on this book you're reading now. And as Ruben described the situation to me, my desire went from zero to negative.

"It's a mess in there," he said. "I have been spraying the place for days and putting out poison. The place is infested with cockroaches and rats." I tried to maintain a positive attitude, but honestly, I wasn't feeling very enthusiastic about the trip.

Ruben is a close friend of mine. We met each other years ago at our parish. He is a family man, a man of prayer, a man of his word – and Ruben is a man of God. As we rolled down the road, I asked him how I might help today. I said I could help with anything – cleaning the house or even helping with Omar's care.

Since I have medical experience, I've pretty much seen it all. I'm not squeamish. Ruben told me that I didn't have to do anything. He said he could manage. But I insisted. "Let me help you. Really, it's no big deal," I said. Then, suddenly, this great big-bear-of-a-man, my friend, broke down and began to cry.

"It's so hard for me," he said, shaking between the tears, "I have to do everything for him. And sometimes he treats me badly. He says terrible things. I'm exhausted. And I'm embarrassed to let you into the house." So right then and there, I backed off. I understood. I just kept driving and listening to my friend vent his anguish.

We drove through the town of Grand Bourg on the outskirts of Buenos Aires, passing through sections of ramshackle houses built with exposed orange blocks and sheets of corrugated tin for roof cover. The occasional horse drawn cart wobbled by, carrying cardboard and rescued junk stacked ten feet high. Youths and children steer these carts through the streets looking for scrap to sell to recycling plants. The urban sprawl of Greater Buenos Aires is immense. Many families down here struggle to make ends meet. Eventually, we pulled up to Omar's place.

Before promising to go with Ruben to visit Omar, I had this week all planned. Like I said, I was going to work on this book. But earlier, while writing, I struggled to find the right work rhythm. I had some ideas, but they seemed stale. The effort felt forced, and it frustrated me. When I heard about Ruben and Omar's situation, I reached out to help. The writing would have to wait.

As we sat out in front of his brother's place, Ruben and I prayed together. Since he didn't want me to come in, I told my friend that I would return to pick him up later. I admit, I was relieved when Ruben didn't let me in. He heaved himself out of my car, opened the rusty gate, and disappeared into the house. And as I drove home, the idea for this book began to unfold in my mind. It all came into place as I was in sync with God. I was in the flow, in the Spirit. I was where I was supposed to be – not necessarily where I wanted to be.

As I write this, these events literally occurred just hours ago. The words are nearly writing themselves. And as more time passed, the entire premise of this book came to me. I feel it was a true revelation from God. This kind of experience is much more common than you might think.

Still, I had to take that step, to help a friend, before it could be shown to me. Many years of experience, study, and prayer were being unlocked and finally taking shape. But first, I had to witness Ruben's valiant struggle – going day-in and day-out to care for his sick brother – before my understanding was opened.

Usually, Ruben takes one-and-a-half hours and three buses to get there and back. This man of God, my friend, had essentially no support in his struggle. He cares for his brother's wounded legs, changes Omar's stained bed sheets, and clears out the rats and the roaches – because that's what Jesus would do.

Later, I went back to pick up Ruben. As I waited outside in the heat, a parrot next door kept calling me, "HOLA! HOLA!" it said. I answered, "Hola!" and so we had a conversation. And then I meditated on things. Finally, Ruben appeared at the door, opened the squeaky gate, and fell into the passenger seat of my car. He looked exhausted.

"I don't want to come here anymore," he groaned. "Every day is a huge struggle. I'm not sure why it has to be this way. I'm not sure if I can take much more. But still, every day, once-a-day, I sit and pray. And God shows me somehow why I'm supposed to be here. That's what keeps me going. God shows me why."

Are you starting to see what I mean? Life is much more than performance optimization and the pursuit of the 'good life'. Instead, it's the Kingdom. It's God's will be done. And it's not all struggle and pain either – there's plenty of celebration and joy too. But some things are painfully hard to accept, no matter how in tune you are with God.

Chapter 2: Early morning & meeting Omar

When I get up, first thing in the morning, I go outside to seek the sun. I look towards the sun (not directly at it!) for about five to six minutes. According to hundreds of research studies, early sunlight viewing is a powerful stimulus for wakefulness throughout the day. Sunlight stimulates your body's cortisol production which helps you face the day with more energy. Research also says it has a powerful and positive impact on your ability to fall and stay asleep at night. It turns out that early daylight impacts your body's melatonin production which helps you sleep better. Just five minutes of looking towards the sun every morning does all that for you. The eye-brain-body connection is truly amazing.

There was a man in history who also got up early every day, even before the sun came up. That man was Jesus of Nazareth. He got up before dawn to seek communion with his Father in heaven. I'm sure Jesus caught many sunrises during his lifetime.

So, as I look towards the sun each morning, I give thanks to God for my own life and the new dawn.

But why even seek the sun? Why pray? Maybe you want more energy. Or you want to have inner peace. You want to be ready. But for what? What do we want these things for? Maybe you want to work more efficiently so you can get things done faster. Or you want to make more money. Perhaps you want to outcompete someone. Is success and efficiency all there is to life? Of course not, but our world is obsessed with these kinds of things.

The number of self-improvement books, experts, and influencers out there is mind boggling. In fact, the U.S. self-improvement industry is expected to balloon to $14 billion within the next few years. What are we all looking for in this relentless quest for self-improvement? I think the answer is simple. We all want to feel good, or at least better. I do too.

So, in pursuit of this effort, I wake up early and seek the sun. I pray. It makes me feel good. But we all know there's more to life than just feeling good. Realities like the one Omar lives – poor health and severe emotional problems – are all too real. No matter how much self-improvement we seek, how can we feel good knowing that our fellow humans suffer so much? I discovered part of the answer when Ruben invited me into Omar's home.

If the other day was hot, today was blazing. The mercury was pushing 100°F (38°C). My plan today was to give Ruben a ride, drop him off at Omar's, and head home. The heat, stress, and lifting Omar's heavy legs made Ruben's back ache terribly. It was obvious he was going through a tough time. As we pulled up to the house, I was hesitant, but I offered to help in any way possible. As my friend got out of the car he said, "Wait for me here. I want to see how things are before I let you in." Did I ask to go in?

So, I waited outside. And ideas filled my head. We sometimes hear or think about God's will. And the idea of life flow, performance, and synchrony with God could be interpreted as doing God's will. It always strikes me though when someone declares, "It's not God's will." How in the world do they know what is or isn't his will?

Typically, people say this when someone does something wrong. Or when a tragedy occurs, we say, "That's not God's will." It's not God's will when a person decides to rebel and sin, we say. Or it's not God's will for you to give into temptation. Some people might say that any kind of sin is not God's will. But I think there's more to it than meets the eye.

What if you chose people for a team you were leading, and one of your team members cheated on you? And what if that betrayal led to harm coming to you, or even to your death? Many of you are already thinking, and you're right – I'm talking about Judas. He was a beloved apostle of Jesus', but Judas eventually turned Jesus over to the authorities.

Did the actions of Judas go against God's will? Were they evil? Did Judas act sinfully? Like I said, God's will is deeply mysterious. When Jesus prayed in Gethsemane, the night prior to his crucifixion, he knew what was coming.

> *And going a little farther he fell on his face and prayed, "My Father, if it be possible, let this cup pass from me; nevertheless, not as I will, but as thou wilt."*

Matthew 26:39

Shortly after his prayer, Judas appeared with the soldiers that would lead Jesus to his death. This was a terrible turn of events. Was it all God's will? And over the centuries there have been countless people who died for their faith. What place does the death of a martyr hold in God's will?

As you can see, God's will isn't always so neat and tidy. It can be hard, complicated, and even brutal sometimes. Does being in the flow apply here too? Perhaps this is where we push beyond the limits of popular modern-day themes like life optimization and self-improvement. If flow is real – or if being in God's will is important – it should apply to every situation, no matter how uncomfortable or extreme.

Ruben suddenly appeared at the door and waved to me. Now I can't compare visiting Omar to facing crucifixion, but I wasn't very enthusiastic about it. I entered the squeaky gate. As we stepped inside, I instinctively held my breath. When I did breathe, there was a powerful smell, like burnt rubber. I heard a deep voice coming from the bedroom. It was Omar calling out to Ruben.

"What's that smell?" Omar asked.

"It's the water pump," Ruben half shouted. "The seal must have worn out, and the pump burned out." And as I turned the corner, I got to see Omar with my own eyes.

He was lying flat, face up on a large bed. Peeling paint hung on the walls. The TV was on. Omar's belly was enormous. He greeted me with a grunt while he looked at me with sleepy eyes. He mumbled something I couldn't understand. The air in the room was thick and humid. The drawn shade made it hard to see. The most striking thing about the scene? Omar's feet and legs. They were swollen to mammoth proportions and covered with thick, gray-purplish, scaly skin. Stained bandages hung loosely around his wrinkled ankles covered with impossibly dense, cracked skin. I'll spare you the details about Omar's puffy feet, toes, and toenails – let your imagination fill in the gaps. Remember when I said I wasn't squeamish? Well, I felt pretty squeamish now.

I took a deep breath and summoned all my courage. I followed Ruben's lead. We proceeded to remove the bandages and wash Omar's legs and feet. Omar and I began to get to know each other.

Chapter 3: We are all wounded

By now you're probably starting to get an idea about the message I'm trying to share. But before we move forward, we should stop and take care of some old business. Being in sync with God, in a heavenly flow, isn't just about helping your neighbor. It's not only about adopting healthy practices. It's more than seeking the sun and praying each morning. I believe living in God's will, under the guidance of his Spirit, requires a fundamental first step. I do not think that anyone can truly advance emotionally, spiritually, and in-step with God until this occurs. What is this all-important process?

We all need to heal our hurt. For me, it's a non-negotiable part of spiritual growth.

No human being exists that hasn't been wounded. Who hasn't been hit, hurt, rejected, or shamed? We've all experienced these things. No one lives a pain free life. And it all began when you were a young child, an infant even. It happened to me too. But as a child, you didn't have the resources to deal with the aggression and stress that appear in life. You didn't know how to get help either. Instead, you may have felt panic or grief. It's like asking a kid to fix a broken water pipe without any tools or experience.

Undoubtedly, painful experiences in your childhood left their mark. It's an open wound you may have carried for years, maybe even your whole life. And as life continued, other trials and tribulations showed up at your door. That's a lot for anyone to deal with. We're all victims of past and present trauma.

For some people, this could explain your lack of motivation. It's not that you are lazy and worthless. Instead, it could be you have old, lasting wounds that need to be healed. Who can move forward when they are in pain? Unfortunately, many self-treat the hurt with alcohol, drugs, being online all the time, or other unhealthy behavior. It's very difficult to break out of these patterns. And without a doubt, healing is essential to achieve lasting, wholesome motivation.

Now don't get me wrong. I don't believe we are all just victims of circumstance. We must accept responsibility for our actions. But when you were just a kid, you were defenseless. Even when you didn't do anything wrong, people hurt you. And that can still happen as an adult. So, if we want to look forward with confidence and hope, if we want to achieve inner harmony with God, we must heal our history first.

In some people, over time, new injuries inflicted upon old wounds lead to inhuman reactions. I remember years ago, someone very close to me mistreated his family. I'll call him X. His behavior was arrogant and selfish. This made me very angry at the time. It seemed X always put his own interests first. And it hurt me. Back then, when I was younger, I didn't have much of a faith-life. I admit, there were times I wished X was dead.

These strong emotions can run through all of us. While it's uncommon to see someone take violent action, it does happen. Or your anger might show itself in other ways, such as a desire to control everything or escape from your responsibilities.

From the depths of our old wounds, many current problems rise to the surface. My anger towards X also spilled over into other relationships. Since there was nothing I could do about X's behavior, it frustrated me. It made me impatient. I remained angry at X for many years, and it created a sore place in my heart. It wasn't until much later that I understood him at a deeper level. Eventually, I realized that X did not love himself at all. Despite his selfish, narcissistic behavior, deep down he had no concept of healthy self-love.

Jesus said, *"You shall love your neighbor as yourself"* (Mark 12:31). But what if you don't love yourself? I believe that without healthy self-love, you can commit any atrocity against someone else – even those closest to you, even your own family. X might have appeared to love himself, but deep down, he didn't understand how to love, at least not in a wholesome way. That's why he mistreated those around him. Once I understood this, it set me free from my anger. No, I don't approve of X's past behavior, not at all. But I'm not angry anymore. I don't wish for his death. Instead, I wish, hope, and pray for his salvation.

What about those who committed the worst acts of evil? What about Adolf Hitler or Joseph Stalin? These men were responsible for the torture and death of millions of men, women, and children. Could past trauma possibly explain the heinous crimes they committed against humanity? It turns out both men were victims of abusive fathers. Also, Hitler's younger brother Edmund died from measles when young Adolf was 11 years old. Did these early childhood traumas eventually drive these men to torture and murder millions? I'm certain their early trauma played a huge role in their behavior later as men. I'm certain X carries old wounds that require healing too.

Why some of us become violent, even murderous, as a response to childhood trauma is a mystery. Still, we all might feel a bit of rage when we see injustice or if someone invades our space. We see how angry we can get when a sensitive subject is brought up. We fly off the handle, and our face transforms. We might yell, slam doors, or even throw things. What explains this explosive behavior? Much of it comes from old wounds that have not yet been healed. If I have a broken bone and you bump it, I'm going to yell. What happens then if I have a broken spirit?

Maybe it was physical abuse. Or maybe you were neglected or ignored. Others were victims of ridicule or abandonment. Trauma is universal, and this is a big reason we see so much behavior that perplexes us. How can someone be so cruel, selfish, or unreasonable? Maybe it's because they've been hurting for so many years, and they haven't learned yet to heal. They haven't learned to love themselves. None of this excuses hurtful or violent behavior. Being a victim doesn't give anybody the right to cause harm to others. But it does help us understand the 'why' behind it all. And this understanding leads us to develop compassion. It also helps us understand our own reactions and our own need for healing.

I've been visiting a prison in Argentina for nearly 10 years now. Every time I visit, I am treated with the utmost respect and hospitality. All the men I visit experienced traumatic pasts. One morning, I was speaking to a group of 12 men. We exchanged jokes and talked about sports and the weather. Some of them were serving very long prison sentences. They had committed a variety of crimes, including violent crime. At one point, our conversation took on a more serious tone.

We all began to open up about our past. I was stunned to hear that all of them, all 12, had been exposed to not only violence as children, but also abandonment. Starting at the age of six, one lived alone in the subway tunnels of Buenos Aires. The mother of another man (he never knew his father) left him behind to be raised by a drunken, heavy-handed uncle. Another lived on the streets nearly all his life. That morning, story after story was told about deep pain and suffering, and the tears began to fall. Yes, these men were criminals. But before they became criminals, they were little boys. And they were all victims of crime. That morning, as we shared our stories, we all experienced a good bit of healing.

You might be thinking, "What does this have to do with me? I'm not a narcissist, tyrant, or criminal." But do you have wounds that need healing? I do. We all do. And sometimes our wounds make us react in unhealthy ways. Maybe you don't lash out or explode, but instead you bottle it all up inside. Some can get resentful or simply just go numb. Others may turn to alcohol or drugs to ease the pain. We look for ways to escape. We may not always be aware of it, but we *all* need healing.

In many ways, I believe our past wounds are the root of all evil. Any maliciousness inflicted upon us is the result of someone else's sin. Some say all the problems and suffering in this world are due to sin. And it makes complete sense. In the Bible, the first murder was Cain killing his brother Abel. Cain was driven by complacency towards God, that is, Cain did not care to give his best. Later, he was driven by envy and resentment towards his brother. So, he killed him. And even until now, the hurt hasn't stopped. I believe we can trace all the pain we see in the world back to that first murder. And it turns out Cain and Abel were the sons of two sinners, Adam and Eve.

We continue to get hurt as life goes on. Even hearing about someone else's pain hurts us. Nobody can escape the news about other people's problems. The digital age has made this even worse as we can see countless images of people getting injured or killed. Wound upon wound continues to pile up. Maybe we go through life acting as if it doesn't affect us. But if that was true, there wouldn't be so much hurt these days. We would all be at peace.

So, we hurt each other, withdraw, or even abuse our bodies trying to ease the pain. We are constantly being wounded, but we must live and carry on at the same time. The best way I have found to deal with this is to ask God to heal me. Sometimes, I just fall to my knees and ask for healing. It might not even be for anything specific. I just know I'm hurting. And I need God's healing grace so very much.

Let's face it, no matter what they say, time alone does not heal all wounds. They can still bleed, hurt, or take forever to scar over. Getting help – such as from psychological counseling or mutual-help groups – can be valuable in the healing process. But we should also include God during our ongoing healing. Many times, Jesus entered people's lives by healing them first. Healing came before any repentance or forgiveness – or healing and forgiving occurred simultaneously. Jesus wants us to be healthy in every way. He healed many physical ailments. And he heals our wounded souls.

When you have an unhealed open inner wound, it's as if the grace of God spills out from the wound – it gets lost somehow. Ironically, the wound is also where God's grace enters to heal. There are some places – deep in our hearts and our history – that can only be reached by God. Why is this? Because he is the only one we can completely trust. So go to the Lord on a regular basis. Ask God for healing. The challenges to come will require the healthiest version of you possible.

BE HEALED

Do you have old wounds that still hurt you? Where does your anger come from? Could your lack of motivation or enthusiasm be due to old wounds? Have you asked God to heal you?

Maybe you don't remember anything specific. But you can still ask the Lord for healing.

Find a quiet place to pray and ask him out loud,

"Heal me, O Lord. Heal me. Heal my wounds."

Sometimes I say this tiny prayer out loud, over and over again. I am so thankful for how God responds.

Chapter 4: Getting to know you

The spiritual life isn't just about healing, carrying your cross, and confronting your inner demons. When seeking harmony with God in your life, there will be times when you actually feel like you're floating on the clouds. I think you know what I mean.

Have you ever experienced moments of sublime grace where even the simplest actions seem supernatural somehow? Basic chores become effortless. Your work flows like a breeze, and even heading out to the corner store feels like an adventure somehow. The world around you comes vibrantly alive, and you appreciate nature and people with fresh eyes.

You find the perfect parking space exactly when you need it. You get everything done right on time. It's kind of like being a superhero cruising effortlessly through life.

Maybe that's how Adam and Eve experienced paradise. Everything is just right, and everything in its proper place. When you can, enjoy these moments to the fullest and praise God all along the way. He's the one who makes everything pleasant in your life at that instant. These moments may not last long, but they should be savored. And don't get sad when these states of higher bliss end – even if they end abruptly.

Keep in mind that a more profound truth is revealed to you during these experiences. Even when you face difficulty, even when you suffer and struggle, you are still on time if you genuinely seek and accept God's will. The reality is, you enter into heavenly timing – since you are on God's time. And on God's time – even if you are hustling to get somewhere – it all seems to fall into place. This took me a long time to understand. And it's not always obvious until you look back.

Living according to God's time and in his will involves your:

- State of mind - You make a conscious effort to consider God throughout the day.
- Attitude - Your desire for contact with God is ingrained in you, but not as an obligation.
- Vision - You see things from a different perspective, a heavenly perspective.
- Spirit - This means your spirit communicates with the Spirit of God. State of mind, attitude, and vision all depend upon this communication.

While none of this comes without some effort, it must be possible. The scriptures are very clear about this:

This is the covenant that I will make with the house
of Israel after those days, says the Lord:
I will put my laws into their minds,
and write them on their hearts,
and I will be their God,
and they shall be my people.
And they shall not teach every one his fellow
or every one his brother, saying, 'Know the Lord,'
for all shall know me,
from the least of them to the greatest.

Hebrews 8:19-11

Nobody can do this perfectly, but we can all grow in getting closer to this state of being. But let's not move too fast forward. We have some things that need our attention first, like getting back to Omar's story.

As the days went on, I edged deeper into Omar's day-to-day care. Even though I have experience as a physician, it was my volunteer work at a hospice that enabled me to help Ruben care for his brother's needs – including bodily hygiene. A hospice is a place where comfort and care are provided to the terminally ill. You see a lot of tough realities at the hospice. Every story is heartbreaking. You quickly learn not to be overwhelmed by what the human body, and spirit, can suffer.

Surprisingly, the hospice I volunteered at (Hospice San Camilo) isn't a place of death. On the contrary, it is a true home that celebrates life, community, and giving. I remember during the pandemic, people were deathly afraid that the virus would rip through the place and take people's lives prematurely. Many volunteers stopped going during the cold winter months. But not a single house guest was infected by Covid during the pandemic – not one.

The place is amazing. Thanks to the loving people that work and volunteer there, many suffering souls have left this world full of peace and joy. I am convinced that Hospice San Camilo is blessed with the powerful presence and protection of God. The hospice's built-in chapel, that houses the Eucharist, is undoubtedly part of the reason why.

The realities of those who come to the hospice aren't easy. Even though I wasn't caring for him at the hospice, Omar's situation ranked up there as one of the most difficult I've ever seen. As we spent more time together, we began to have heart-to-heart conversations.

"I always lived live by the motto 'mierda o plata' (sh*t or money)," Omar said, sitting on the edge of his bed, gazing out the window. "I would go all in, all the time. Money or nothing." Now, bedridden, with a failing heart and lungs, his body reflected that Omar hadn't come out on the money side.

Historically, Argentina is a Catholic nation. Many evangelical churches have also thrived down here. In recent years, however, many Christians of all denominations have fallen away from their faith in this country. Nevertheless, Argentina is largely a nation of believers in God, and over the last 20 years living down here, I've witnessed tremendous levels of faith in this fascinating land.

"I don't believe in God. Nope. When I was a kid, catechism was the worst. So boring and dull," Omar moaned. He told me he believes in energies and the force-of-will as a life philosophy. While he spoke to me, I put on latex gloves to lift his heavy, bandaged legs so he could lie down in bed.

"Maybe you didn't like catechism because they taught you about Jesus as a subject matter – rather than teaching you about the Man. If your teachers did not have a personal relationship with Jesus, then it would have been impossible to transmit the true essence of Christ to you," I told him as I adjusted his bed sheets. Omar answered me with silence. Thinking.

What difference does it make in my life whether Jesus is who he said he was? Why should we even ask the question? Is it really that important? The truth is that Jesus made so many outlandish claims that his relevance – even today – urges us to look for answers. If you stop and think about it, Jesus' claim that he was God's Son is earth shattering. If God exists, and he sent his Son, doesn't that make it the most important event in human history? Doesn't that make it the most important event in my history and yours?

Back in the time when the Gospel events took place, this kind of talk – saying that you were God's son – was considered blasphemy. This meant that it was a statement directly against God. It was like throwing mud or something worse at him. What would drive a man – especially a wise and compassionate man –

to make such a claim that was punishable by death? Why didn't he just stop at saying we should be good, merciful, and kind? Why did Jesus have to say he was God's Son? What purpose did it serve?

Many people are misled when it comes to what Christianity is all about. They mistakenly think it means that you must be good. This is what I call the "Good Guy Gospel" which really has nothing to do with the Gospel of Jesus Christ. While one of the results of being a Christian is improved behavior and attitudes, it's not the central message. Instead, it has to do with Jesus' identity and mission.

This brings us to a critical concept: it's not good conduct that makes you a Christian. You are a Christian when you believe that God forgives you and loves you – all perfectly revealed in God's son Jesus Christ. The weight of this distinction is enormous.

Every great religion offers us some kind of liberation. They all seduce us with the chance of being happy and fulfilled. Each one suggests that we can find some meaning in our lives. But all of them, except one, start by giving us a list – large or small – of things we must do. Only Jesus offers us what he did for us first. True Christianity is not belief in a set of rules or doctrine, but faith in a person instead.

So now, inevitably, we come to the sticky issue of sin. Even the word itself irritates some people. They just can't accept it, and unfortunately, it's partly the Christians' fault – at least the fault of Christians that believe in the Good Guy Gospel. For far too many years, and far too many times, we have attempted to establish the criteria for who gets into heaven. We sit in judgment and decide who's naughty and nice. So, we pressure everyone – especially ourselves – into being good.

This happens in every Christian denomination. Even if they say it doesn't, the Good Guy Gospel somehow sneaks in there. Whether we admit it or not, part of us might think that we can buy our way into heaven with good conduct alone. We then insist that

31

others accept this as the only way to salvation. I've adopted this attitude many times. I've offended myself, my family, and my God with this mistake. And every time he reminds me of the same thing.

He tells me, "Please stop. Please stop trying to be the one who decides who I accept, forgive, and love. Please stop trying to work your way into my good graces. It just doesn't work that way. Don't you understand? It is I who does the work. It's my Son who paid the price. You can't do it."

"But God," I reply. "I want to make it better. I want to do the right thing. I want to be good!"

And God answers: "Don't worry but rest, my child. Rest in the fact that I am the one that will make it all better. Quit trying to buy your way into salvation. Once and for all, just let it go. Give all your pain, suffering, and sin up to me and my Son. Just accept, once and for all, that I love you as you are. And my loving Spirit will change you."

And so, I remember that I'm human. I make mistakes. Just my thoughts are horrible sometimes. It means that I'm a sinner, as we all are. If anything, this makes us all equal. Many people think that evil is due to oppression, religion, government, or some other external factor. But the reality is that we're all fully capable of creating our own tragedy. I have five kids and nearly 50 nieces and nephews. I've seen infants act in cruel and selfish ways. Some say it's the influence of modern society, but a leading cause of death – even in isolated, primitive tribes – is murder.

God knows your heart. You and I know who we are. Sure, we can be good, but we can be downright terrible too. Just look at our world, look at the headlines, and you can see our downfall. Economically, politically, socially, morally – the world's leaders have all fallen in some way or another, just like us. So how do we reconcile the bad parts of us? How do we begin to make amends? Where do we find perfect justice?

We can know a man is guilty of a crime and condemn him. But what about the family that neglected or abused the man as a boy, or the society that looked the other way when he needed help or guidance? Where do we find perfect justice for all the bad things that happen? The reality is that we can't, at least not on our own. We can't even come close.

When I came to Jesus, I was carrying a lot of psychological and emotional baggage. In many ways, like Omar, I also had lived a life of 'mierda o plata'. The burden of my mistakes was overwhelming. Yes, I tried to be better, but better wasn't enough. Trying to make amends is not the same as being able to stand in God's presence with confidence in his love. This confidence does not come from any good deeds on my part. Instead, I need his help.

Jesus, if he is really God's son – that makes me sit up and take notice. And if God's Son died for me… well, that leaves me astounded. And the full impact of this – if you let it reach your heart – can transform your entire existence.

Chapter 5: Spiritual combat

I felt terrible anguish. Horrific images flashed in my mind. Omar's huge, disfigured body. The gray, cracked, scaly skin on his swollen legs and feet. The darkness invading his room. Seeing things that nobody should ever have to see. Touching things that nobody should ever have to touch. I tossed and turned in bed. The images stuck in my head, and I could not shake them. The night seemed to drag on forever.

Who did I think I was, some kind of hero? What in the world was I doing getting involved with Ruben's problems? It ended up that I had been going every morning to help care for his brother. Sometimes I even went alone. Sure, Ruben is my friend and brother in faith, but did I have to commit so much time and effort to helping him? What if I went to Omar's house one morning and found him dead on the floor? And the enemy kept telling me that I'm a fool.

The accuser whispered to me over and over again, "It's only going to get worse. This will never end. Don't you think Omar would be better off dead? Don't you wish he would just die? Then you can be free." These wicked thoughts twisted around my worry.

I felt a choking sensation. But what would Ruben do if I didn't help him? How much could my friend endure before he cracks?

This is a classic example of a spiritual fight. It's worry or pain driving your thoughts to where you feel out of control. All kinds of strange sensations and temptations come boiling to the surface. You feel like you want to run away and hide. Or you might feel an urgency to do something, anything. And many times, the last thing you want to do is pray. Understanding spiritual combat is essential to knowing how to stay in sync with God.

As I wrestled with my thoughts that night, other worries came rushing in like ghosts – concerns about my family, the future, and even our pet dog. It's almost as if your entire existence comes crumbling down around you. You think everything's a mess, and you'll never be able to fix it all. The enemy rejoices when he sees you tangled up like this in anguish. It's a free fall into the bottomless chaos of your mind. You feel like there's no hope for tomorrow. And the loss of hope is the devil's victory.

So what can defeat the enemy? What drives the accuser away from you? What does Satan hate? He hates calm. He despises peace. In my case, the evil one vanished when I pulled myself out of bed, fell to my knees, and prayed.

"O merciful Lord, help me. Stand. Fight for me! Help me Jesus. I can't do any of this on my own. It's impossible."

And with this simple confession of fragility – admitting full dependence on God – the evil one left me. By simply stating that I don't have all the answers, I was set free. As my soul confessed that I needed God's help, my mind was set at ease. When we pray, God provides his clarity and calm, and the enemy cannot tolerate the presence of peace.

Today's modern reality is super complex. There are so many moving parts. New layers of decision-making keep getting added to everyday life. We're all trying to adjust, but it stresses us out because we feel like we can't keep up sometimes. And the world stirs up conflicting dialogs inside us. We hear dozens of opinions

– about health, race, politics, and religion – and we can't fit all the pieces into the puzzle. Everyone's brain fizzles a bit these days.

Then something happens, maybe a major crisis or a loss hits home. We reach our limit, and we're tempted to lose hope. We worry ourselves in circles instead of seeking God. It's at those times when you must grit your teeth, pull yourself up, and dig into prayer. The enemy will throw everything he can at you to stop this from happening. Every tiny concern grows into a scary giant. These moments can be incredibly intense. It is a true fight, even brutal sometimes. But when you give in and give it all up to God, the heavens open up to you. And almighty God takes over the fight.

In those moments of combat and prayer, fundamental truths are revealed to you. You don't deny the chaos and friction, but it doesn't consume you either. You learn to let go of your anger or fear. Hope is restored, and it's miraculous. No, your reality doesn't change at that instant, but God focuses your heart and mind. You accept that you don't have all the answers. And in the middle of your doubts and fears, your faith grows stronger. As you continue to pray, the obstacles in your mind come tumbling down. You rest in Him. Then you can continue forward with confidence.

You might pray something like this…

> *"Lord, I will not walk without you. I need you. Rise*
> *up. Cast out the evil one. Defend me!"*

These are miracle making words. They are based on profound trust in God. And these words have great power when it comes to spiritual combat.

Still, this isn't the only type of spiritual battle. Those tough moments, when you face your limits, are actually part of much larger campaigns, and the bigger picture might not be what you imagine. It's not all about demons and evil spirits. Instead, the real fight is much more down to earth.

The idea of spiritual combat has been made popular by sensationalists and religious denominations for years. Motion pictures add to the hype. What is spiritual combat then? Is it fighting against the devil and black magic? Is it about rallying against the forces of evil at work in society? Many who talk about spiritual combat might not fully grasp the true struggle that takes place every day in heaven and on earth.

Some might fight within a religious context, but they might lose ground in the more important spiritual war. And this can lead to serious problems. So what's the key mistake we want to avoid? Problems occur when we place too much emphasis on the external. That is, sometimes we're too busy fixing things on the outside, but our inner lives are a mess.

One example is the debate over abortion. Every life is unique and unrepeatable – yours, mine, everyone's. Every life is precious and should be protected from the moment of conception. But some people turn their anti-abortion stance into a crusade of manipulation or control. Or maybe they just want attention. Meanwhile, they bully, harass, or even threaten people to get their way. They might even make a lot of money from the effort. Or they become one-dimensional figures instead of human beings. They might alienate people, and this behavior spills over into other areas of their life. So, while the cause (protecting the unborn child) may be noble, the inner spiritual battle is lost. Any worship of a cause is just another form of idolatry.

Meanwhile, others think spiritual combat is only about casting out demons through exorcisms or liberation ministries. Yes, it's true that demonic forces can wreak havoc in people's lives. If you leave the door open, nasty things can invade your life. But to be truly effective in the delicate activity of spiritual liberation, a more basic struggle must be mastered first. Again, on the outside we might think we're fighting a spiritual battle, but on the inside, Satan might be winning the war. But if it's not fighting for a worthy cause or casting out demons, what is spiritual combat?

In a nutshell, it's your life testimony.

Think about what might work against you spiritually. What's the best way to give the enemy an advantage? You lose when you don't live by your convictions. You lose when you don't live by truth. If you say, "God is love," but your behavior is contaminated with anger or resentment, then you've already lost the battle. If you make excuses for a bad character, then the enemy wins. If you manipulate religion for the sake of personal glory, power, or financial gain, then the devil jumps for joy. You may achieve some external victories, but you know in your heart that something isn't right. Others can sense it too. If we provide a bad testimony, we set a poor example for others. And this leads to a continuous spread of negative forces.

Now don't get me wrong. It's not about acting good; it's about being good. Your inner spiritual life will inevitably be expressed in your real life. No, you can't win heaven just by good behavior. You will never reach perfection. But it should be easy to discern a life full of the Holy Spirit. When the mercy and love of Christ are at the center, everything else flows from that life giving source.

Make no mistake, this is true spiritual combat. It doesn't get any harder than this. It's not easy to resist something when "everyone does it", even though it's wrong. It's hard to face our selfishness, especially when we think we aren't selfish at all. It may be difficult to resist joining an angry mob that appears to agree with your convictions. It wasn't easy for Jesus to go to the cross. It wasn't easy for him to forgive his killers that crucified him. But with these observable actions, Jesus' testimony laid the foundation for the greatest spiritual victory of all time.

Your testimony is revealed, therefore, in the concrete actions of your everyday life. It's showing up on time. It's being loyal and doing your part. It's being where you are supposed to be when you are supposed to be there. And your testimony when nobody is looking is the critical piece of the puzzle. Leading a double life equals corruption and lies. And any hidden motive or dishonesty translates into a spiritual loss. A huge part of faith is being faithful.

The ability to say 'no' is an all-important weapon. Remember when Jesus faced Satan in the desert? The evil one offered Jesus many temptations, but the Lord resisted. He stood his ground. He didn't give in to desires of the flesh, worldly power, or an easy way out. Instead, he remained faithful in his worship of God. Due to Jesus' obedience and humility – and through his testimony – the Holy Spirit was revealed in the fullest expression possible.

Now, if you struggle with hidden harmful activity, don't give up. There is always hope. If anything, God's message is this: there is always a chance to change. As long as you live and breathe, you can try again. God will always forgive you and receive you. It could be drugs, alcohol, pornography, infidelity, greed… when your heart is divided, you know it. But remember this: your sin is not you.

Do not confuse your identity with the action. Instead, take a look at what's going on with an attentive mind and heart. And invoke God's Spirit to give you the conviction and strength to overcome the challenge. Appeal to his goodness. This may require going back for even deeper healing first. And even if you fail again and again, don't give up trying. Hold on tight to God. In your effort, nothing goes to waste as the Lord forms your character along the way.

From a solid testimony, many blessings come forth. When you share your belief in Jesus, you are credible. People listen. When you are out there serving your neighbor, it inspires others to serve as well. People notice. When mistakes happen, you ask for forgiveness, or you forgive. People value this. What they really see isn't just you, but the Spirit of God working in you and through you. This is the best way to win the spiritual war against evil.

Make no mistake, the battle is fierce. It can be messy, even bloody sometimes. You may feel a burning in your chest or a knot in your throat at times. But be careful not to choose the wrong fight. Don't get distracted by culture wars and campaigns that have nothing to do with your life. Instead, seek to root out the corruption on the inside. Stop taking the easy way out. Stop taking advantage of something dishonest because everyone does it. Don't compromise your convictions, strengthen them instead. Take full charge of your responsibilities and stand your ground. And once that battle is fully fought, others will unfold before you.

Like Jesus, don't fear journeying into the desert to prepare yourself. Win the inner war first, then go out to the world. The battles you win – and even the ones you lose – will give you strength and courage to face greater challenges. The choices you make are what matters. Your convictions will be tested when it truly hits home and exposes your deepest motives. Money, family, work, status... many temptations are found there. Read that last sentence again. Think about how each one might affect your actions. Then learn how to rely on heavenly forces to be victorious.

And pray hard. Remember, the battle is fought on your knees. Then afterwards, in your everyday life, the victories are realized. There is no way around this. Without prayer, without communion with God the Father, there is no way to grow spiritually. There might be good people out there that never pray. But if you believe in the God of Abraham, Isaac, and Jacob – if you believe in the Son of God, Jesus Christ – and if you desire his Holy Spirit to fill your life – then you must pray. Your strength as a spiritual warrior comes from this. Ask the Lord to help you trust more and love more. Pray for the Holy Spirit to heal, free, and fill you with his presence.

If prayer is the spiritual exercise that prepares us for the struggle, then God's Word is the fuel we need to remain strong. Study the scriptures to understand what God shows us about holiness, justice, and mercy.

Finally, your good conduct is not a reason to place yourself on a pedestal. You don't rise above everyone else to be judge and jury about human behavior. That's not what it's about. Instead, it's coming down lower, like God did when he became man. He lowered himself to our level, eye to eye. He came down to heal and to serve. Jesus came down to share the Good News and wash the feet of sinners, even of those who would betray him. And upon this powerful, impeccable testimony, the authority of Christ was established for all eternity.

FIGHT THE GOOD FIGHT

Do you have trouble maintaining a solid life testimony? Are you engaged in conduct that you know isn't healthy for you? Ask the Lord for his help. Ask him to give you a solid testimony. Do not fear the spiritual battle. Take courage. Yes, it can be tough. It requires sacrifice. But it's worth it.

This is an ongoing process. You will lose some fights, but this can be used to your advantage when you seek the Lord's restoration. You grow stronger when you grow more dependent on God.

Spiritual battles must be waged with prayer. There is no way to win without prayer. And when entire communities struggle together, the victories are even greater.

> *Jesus answered them, "I told you, and you do not believe. The works that I do in my Father's name, they bear witness to me.*

John 10:25

The verse above speaks about the importance of your personal testimony.

> *Do not be overcome by evil, but overcome evil with good.*

Romans 12:21

41

Chapter 6: The narrowest gate

In the last chapter we explored what we all experience during our life struggles. We learned that our testimony is the key. But there's another level of spiritual combat that only a few will ever know. Their testimonies can teach us deep secrets about being in tune with God. We should not fear their stories, no matter how difficult they are to hear.

In our modern world, we're tempted to take the sting out of the Gospel message. We want to water it down to make things more inviting. Yes, peace and love are essential, but they don't come easily. Everything of great value requires effort and sacrifice.

Jesus attracted people to him, but he never forced or frightened anyone into believing. Still, the full message of the Gospel must include the cross. It's a truly terrible moment to be considered seriously. But if we trust in God, the cross should not frighten us. Instead, we trust that it leads us to a new dawn.

I won't lie to you. My experience helping care for Omar wasn't enjoyable. I did not look forward to going to his place. The sights, smells, and sounds were highly unpleasant. But the testimonies of countless others tower over my experience.

You won't hear much about it in the mainstream news. They may not even talk about it in our churches. But every year, thousands of Christians, from different denominations, are persecuted or killed for their beliefs. Think about what it would be like if going to church on Sunday put your life at risk.

Consider this story. On June 5, 2022, an attack took place at the St. Francis Xavier Catholic Church in the city of Owo, Nigeria. As worshippers inside the church were celebrating Pentecost, a group of gunmen, disguised as congregants, entered with bags full of weapons. Another group took positions outside the church. At 11:30 am, explosive devices were detonated outside the church, and the gunmen began firing.

Attackers outside the church shot into it while those disguised as congregants fired at the people inside. A boy selling candy at the entrance was shot. Gunmen locked the main doors. They shot anyone who moved. Videos showed bodies of victims lying in pools of blood on the church floor. At least 40 people were killed that day and scores more injured. The attack was driven by hatred for worshippers of Jesus. Incidents like this translate the idea of spiritual combat into very real terms.

Other stories that stand out include what I call the "spontaneous martyrs". These people didn't practice their faith much, or maybe not even at all. They might have come from a Christian family, but they didn't go to church. Then suddenly, they are ripped from their homes by Islamic extremists.

For some reason, a handful of these lukewarm Christians – who never really embraced their faith – refuse to deny their Christian identity at that critical moment. And they face execution. They give their lives for Jesus in that instant. What makes this happen? Why the sudden indomitable faithfulness? The only explanation I can find is a massive outpouring of the Holy Spirit over them right then and there.

A spontaneous conviction in the face of death – what is this experience like? I'm not sure I even want to imagine it. But these incredible events happen in modern times. What does this say to the rest of us?

Some claim the Western world is moving towards the persecution of Christians. Will it reach a point where people are executed for being a believer in Topeka, Montreal, Paris, or London? I doubt it, but persecution in other forms exists. Our convictions are tested more and more each day. On the social, political, and personal level, all believers are being challenged.

How many compromises do I make? On the job? In the public square? At home? In my heart? How many times do I put my interests before God's will in my life? How often do I take the easy way out? Am I skipping time spent seeking God? Do I excuse my bad behavior instead of trusting that God can change me? How many times do I ignore people when I think there's no hope for them?

You might be saying, "Hey, I feel bad for those poor souls. I really do. But I have my own problems. What can I possibly do about those situations? It's all very far away from me."

Believe it or not, there is something you can do. What is it? You can honor those slain for their faith. Most of us (depending on where you live) will never have our lives threatened due to religious persecution. But how often do we shrink down when facing much smaller challenges? We retreat to safety when confronted about our beliefs. Or worse, maybe nobody even knows we believe at all.

I'm not saying we should seek death, but are we living our faith as if our lives depend on it? What if we take the time to reflect upon the risks some face simply by going to church? What might the Spirit show us? Maybe we will cherish our faith and blessings more. Maybe we will embrace our testimony with more authenticity and courage. And when that happens, I'm sure the martyrs in heaven will celebrate joyously.

Consider this passage from scripture:

When he opened the fifth seal, I saw under the altar the souls of those who had been slain for the word of God and for the witness they had borne; they cried out with a loud voice, "O Sovereign Lord, holy and true, how long before thou wilt judge and avenge our blood on those who dwell upon the earth?"

Revelation 6:9-10

Now, there is another group of people that I hesitate to write about. I can only write about them at some risk, since there is no way for me to fully understand their struggle. I pray that nothing I write here causes any of them harm. But I believe their stories must be told.

There are people out there facing unimaginable difficulty every single day. I would not even be able to budge the cross they carry. It might be an illness or a complex family issue. They suffer from serious physical or emotional pain. Or they live under oppressive political regimes. I've received many prayer requests from people living in situations where there is literally no way out.

What do you do when you have a disabled child, and you must live with verbally abusive relatives since you can't afford your own place? What do you do when your son is in jail for drug charges, your crippling arthritis hardly lets you move, and you're about to be evicted from your home? What do you do when you live with a narcissist, and you have no social life, no job, and no family to turn to? And what do you do if you are a child digging with your bare hands in the cobalt mines of the Congo for two dollars a day?

These realities reach the limit of most people's understanding. But many people live like this. Too many. And nobody pays attention. These people should seek and receive help at all costs. But sometimes it's not possible. Sometimes they have no options. And in these cases, the only comfort might be the Lord Jesus Christ, the Creator of the universe, the Lamb of God – if he came for anyone, he came for them. He came especially for those that suffer most.

Jesus identifies in a special way with those that live with deep hurt and pain. He knows what it's like to pay the price for someone else's sin. He knows exactly what it feels like to be betrayed and denied, even by close friends. And he knows how much it hurts to be crucified when you are innocent.

There is no way to justify when people get hurt due to abuse, neglect, or inhuman circumstances. But these souls know Jesus unlike any other. They may be the best representation of Jesus on this earth. They are the face of the suffering God. As for the rest of us, he calls us to help them. So, if you know of a situation like this, go. Go and serve your suffering neighbor as if you are serving the Lord Jesus himself.

And remember, just because others suffer more, that doesn't minimize your suffering. You don't have to face a life-threatening situation to feel the pain. The mercy of the Lord is wide open and spacious. In our suffering, we too can identify with Christ. And if we help others that suffer, we can serve Jesus. We can join with his Spirit to bring healing and comfort to the wounded of the world.

Enter by the narrow gate; for the gate is wide and the way is easy, that leads to destruction, and those who enter by it are many. For the gate is narrow and the way is hard, that leads to life, and those who find it are few.

Matthew 7:13-14

Chapter 7: Knowing yourself

Until now, we've explored some key principles essential to living a life in tune with God. We've talked about things like healing and spiritual combat. Now, we're going to dig even deeper. It's time to dive into other critical aspects of God-centered spiritual harmony. And to do this, we'll look at the lives of some of the greatest spiritual masters of all time. Ironically, some of these figures didn't start out seeking communion with God at all.

What comes to mind when you picture a humble person? Some people might think being humble means being quiet or keeping a low profile. You might imagine someone who is economically poor as being humble. While these might be some examples of humility, I think other definitions are closer to the truth. And humility may be the single most important characteristic we need to be in tune with God.

Try this one on for size: humility is freedom from pride or arrogance. While this definition is more precise, it's still a mostly secular explanation. How can we move deeper into the spiritual meaning of humility? Maybe we can start by looking at the life of a man that was humbler than anyone else in his time. To do this, we must travel back many centuries to meet him.

> *Now Moses was a very humble man, more humble than anyone else on the face of the earth.*
>
> Numbers 12:3

As for myself, I am not naturally humble. I struggle with my vanity and pride. I don't like it, but I know this to be true. Sometimes I'm ashamed to admit it. When it comes to being prideful, there are some people worse than me and some better. Perhaps part of my arrogance was programmed into me as a youth, but most of my lack of humility falls squarely on my shoulders. Maybe you struggle with this too.

What about Moses? Was he ever prideful or arrogant? Even though he was the son of Hebrew slaves, Moses was also the adopted grandson of Pharaoh – one of the most powerful leaders on earth at the time. This means young Moses grew up in the lap of luxury, and he received a prince's education. Later, Moses had to escape from Egypt since he killed an Egyptian. Then after spending 40 years living in the wilderness as a shepherd, God eventually called Moses to return to Egypt to lead the Israelites out of bondage. As the leader of the Israelites, Moses won epic victories over rival nations, and he eventually became the lawgiver and judge over all of Israel.

The drama surrounding Moses' life is astounding. Still, even though he was a larger-than-life prophet, the scriptures say Moses was humble. How can a prince of Egypt and the leader of a conquering nation possibly be humble?

It's been said that Moses was humble since he obeyed God. Yes, obedience can be the result of humility, but some people only obey out of obligation. So, what really made Moses humble? What made him tick? I believe it started with Moses coming to know who he really was, deep inside.

Shortly before Moses was born, Egypt experienced a period of great societal upheaval, and the firstborn children of Israel faced great danger. The Egyptian rulers felt threatened by the growing Hebrew population, so Pharaoh commanded that all male infants be put to death. Moses, a Hebrew, miraculously escaped this horrific decree and was eventually taken in to live as Egyptian royalty (see Exodus 1 & 2).

Even though he lived a protected and privileged life in the house of Pharaoh, Moses could not deny his roots. One day, he went out to see his people toiling away at hard labor under the scorching sun. And when the future prophet saw an Egyptian beating a Hebrew, Moses struck down the Egyptian and killed him.

> *He looked this way and that, and seeing no one,*
> *he killed the Egyptian and hid him in the sand.*

> Exodus 2:12

Even though he could have denied his identity, something inside Moses drove him to want to defend his people. He could have remained indifferent to the suffering of the Hebrew slaves. Moses could have stayed in the comfortable house of Pharoah, but he couldn't deny the truth forever. Still, when Moses took matters into his own hands, through violence, it ended badly. Later, when he tried to settle a dispute between two Hebrews, they revealed his mistake to him.

> *When he went out the next day, behold, two Hebrews*
> *were struggling together; and he said to the man that did*
> *the wrong, "Why do you strike your fellow?" He answered,*
> *"Who made you a prince and a judge over us? Do you mean*
> *to kill me as you killed the Egyptian?" Then Moses was*
> *afraid, and thought, "Surely the thing is known." When*
> *Pharaoh heard of it, he sought to kill Moses.*

> Exodus 2:13-15

Fearing for his life, Moses fled to the desert. There he encountered the daughters of a shepherd priest in Midian. Moses married one of the daughters and started his own family. Then for 40 years he lived as a shepherd, far from the painful memories of Egypt.

> *And Moses was content to dwell with the man, and he gave Moses his daughter Zipporah. She bore a son, and he called his name Gershom; for he said, "I have been a sojourner in a foreign land. In the course of those many days the king of Egypt died. And the people of Israel groaned under their bondage, and cried out for help, and their cry under bondage came up to God."*
>
> Exodus 2:21-23

The story could have easily ended there. Moses could have lived the rest of his days as a shepherd, raising his family in Midian. Instead, God was preparing a new beginning and a far greater plan to liberate an entire nation. So much had happened to Moses already, but his life journey was just getting started.

We can only imagine what Moses meditated on during all those years as a shepherd. He certainly had plenty of time to think about his life up until that point. What did his experience tell him about himself? What conclusions unfolded in his heart and mind all those years tending sheep in the wilderness? What happened next, however, would expand his understanding to a level that Moses could never have imagined.

It all began when Moses encountered God in the burning bush on Mount Horeb. From a distance, Moses saw the bush burning, but it did not get consumed by the fire. Out of curiosity, he moved closer to the bush, and there Moses encountered God in a personal and astounding way.

God called to him out of the bush, "Moses, Moses!"
And he said, "Here am I." Then he said, "Do not come
near; put off your shoes from your feet, for the place on
which you are standing is holy ground." And he said, "I am
the God of your father, the God of Abraham, the God of
Isaac, and the God of Jacob." And Moses hid his face, for
he was afraid to look at God.

Exodus 3:4b-6

In God's presence, everything changes. On holy ground, everything becomes transparent. At that moment, Moses showed how he knew himself. He hid his face in fear. And when the Lord told Moses that he was chosen to lead the Israelites out of bondage, he asked God, *"Who am I that I should go to Pharaoh and bring the Israelites out of Egypt?"* (Exodus 3:11).

Did Moses think he was unqualified now since he was just a simple shepherd? Perhaps Moses felt guilty for his past life of luxury in Pharaoh's house while his fellow Israelites lived as slaves. Or maybe Moses remembered how his attempt to defend the Hebrews backfired. Surely a fugitive murderer couldn't be a leader for the God of Abraham, Isaac, and Jacob. Later, Moses admitted other shortcomings, like his difficulty speaking. *"I am slow of speech and tongue,"* he said (Exodus 4:10).

To be humble, you must know yourself. But sometimes it's hard to face yourself honestly. It can be embarrassing. When we are brutally honest with ourselves, it's humiliating. I know I have experienced this. And many times, God – and other people – have shown me where I'm not doing so great. I've had to ask for forgiveness many times. So, humility starts by knowing yourself and not fearing the truth.

The alternative is to hide behind a false image of yourself. Or maybe you *do* know yourself, but you minimize things. One of the biggest tricks we play on ourselves is when we say "that's just the way I am" which slams the door shut on change. Or we use the "at least I'm not as bad as so-and-so" excuse. But this comparison is dangerous. There's always someone worse than us, and at the end of the line stands the devil himself.

When these defense mechanisms are challenged, our pride and arrogance rise up. We make excuses for bad behavior or ignore it – and humility escapes us. Still, deep down we know the truth, and we feel out of sync with ourselves. And when we are out of sync with ourselves, we're out of tune with God. But if we watch ourselves and listen to others, we can admit our faults.

. . . .

Be honest with yourself.

Is there something about yourself you wish you could change?

Ask God to show you how. Don't be afraid.

In prayer, you enter holy ground. There God reveals the truth to you.

Be patient with yourself, but also have faith that God can and will help you.

Yes, the Lord loves you as you are – but he wants you to be better, healthier, and free.

Chapter 8: Knowing God

Humility doesn't end with knowing yourself. It's not only about recognizing your faults. The truly humble also seek to know God. When the Lord told Moses to return to Egypt, the prophet wanted to know more.

> *Moses said to God, "If I come to the people of Israel and say to them, 'The God of your fathers has sent me to you,' and they ask me, 'What is his name?' what shall I say to them?" God said to Moses, "I AM WHO I AM." And he said, "Say this to the people of Israel, 'I AM has sent me to you.'"*

Exodus 3:13-14

From that moment, a lifelong relationship began. We know Moses talked to God on many occasions after that day on Mount Horeb. In Exodus 33 it says, *"Thus the Lord used to speak to Moses, face to face, as a man speaks to his friend."*

Imagine those conversations! One of the greatest prophets ever, chatting with the Creator of the universe. What did they talk about? We know Moses consulted with the Lord about many important decisions. The prophet-leader did not depend on his own insight alone, even though he had plenty of experience. Moses knew that his own strength and knowledge would never be enough to free the Hebrew slaves.

God gave Moses direct guidance about how to lead the nation of Israel. Sometimes he gave Moses highly detailed instructions, such as the contents of the Ten Commandments. But I'm sure God and Moses talked about other things as well – things not written in the scriptures. It says they spoke to each other as friends. What do friends talk about?

Moses must have praised God many times during their talks. I imagine after being freed from Egypt, or after a great victory, or when God provided Manna from heaven for the hungry people to eat, Moses must have shown God his appreciation. I'm sure Moses gave God thanks and praise. But the prophet also complained bitterly to God. He freely expressed his frustration and anguish, and Moses even threatened to throw in the towel many times. He even went so far as to question God's motives.

After the burning bush episode, Moses came down from Mount Horeb, and he set out for Egypt. Then Moses went to Pharaoh and demanded that he let the people go. But Pharaoh did not respect Moses, and he did not respect God either.

> *But Pharaoh said, "Who is the Lord, that I should heed his voice and let Israel go? I do not know the Lord, and moreover I will not let Israel go."*

Exodus 5:2

Full of pride, Pharoah did not know God. Unlike Moses, the Egyptian didn't care to get to know the Lord either. Then Pharoah made things even worse for the Hebrews. He sent out a decree saying that the slaves had to gather their own straw to make bricks. This made the work much harder. But the number of bricks made per day could not decrease, and the slave drivers beat the Israelites.

Inevitably, they complained about the new harsh brick making standards. Moses complained too.

> *Then Moses turned again to the Lord and said, "O Lord, why hast thou done evil to this people? Why didst thou ever send me? For since I came to Pharaoh to speak in thy name, he has done evil to this people, and thou hast not delivered thy people at all."*
>
> Exodus 5:22-23

True friends talk like this. Friends might even fight with each other sometimes. There's no acting involved. They put their hearts on the table without fear. Moses had no problem being sincere with God thanks to a deep bond of trust. No matter what, a true friendship has a profound effect on you.

Have you ever noticed that when you spend a lot of time with someone, you pick up their mannerisms? You might begin to talk like them and even act like them a bit. When people move to another country, they frequently adopt the local accent. When you are in contact with someone for a long time, they rub off on you. That's what happened to Moses. God rubbed off on him – and this made Moses humble. He was reminded about God's identity. And the Lord continued to guide the prophet into understanding a much bigger picture of things to come.

> *And God said to Moses, "I am the Lord. I appeared to Abraham, to Isaac, and to Jacob, as God Almighty... Say therefore to the people of Israel, 'I am the Lord, and I will bring you out from under the burdens of the Egyptians, and I will deliver you from their bondage, and I will redeem you with an outstretched arm and with great acts of judgment, and I will take you for my people, and I will be your God...'*
>
> Exodus 6:2-3a, 6-7a

Being in contact with God and talking to him helps us tremendously. For me, this was my only chance at achieving some level of humility. Many times, he showed me when I was going down the wrong path or when I expressed unhealthy attitudes. He listened to my frustrations and anxieties. And if needed, he gave me a hard stop before it was too late.

This process of purification happens to absolutely everyone who genuinely seeks communion with God. It doesn't make you perfect. You still make mistakes. But the Lord helps you avoid the big errors that carry a heavy price. The more time you spend with God, the more you know what he wants for you and from you. Then you don't have to hide behind the masks of pride and fear anymore. You feel safe and sure with God as your friend.

In this process, God also reveals a bigger picture to you, just like he did with Moses. He shows you his heavenly, glorious plan. It can be hard to understand and accept sometimes, but the humble heart listens and receives God's will. Your understanding grows. Your perspective deepens. And as you walk with God along the path of humility, you come to realize that it's not all about you.

Chapter 9: Humbly stand up

Moses worked hard for the people of Israel. The responsibility of an entire nation rested on his shoulders. He must have faced intense moments of stress and worry. Leadership might not instantly make you think about humility, but the best leaders are truly humble. And the episode we are about to hear about in Moses's life might surprise you in how humility can be manifested.

The Lord sent Moses several times to command Pharoah to let the people go, but the Egyptian hardened his heart each time. So, the Lord sent ten devastating plagues upon the land of Egypt – water turned to blood, frogs, lice, flies, pestilence, boils, hail, locusts, darkness, and finally the worst of all, the death of the Egyptian firstborn. When we harden our hearts against God, serious consequences follow.

Eventually, Pharoah did let the people go, but his heart was so hard that he chased the Israelites into the desert. Finally, they came to the Red Sea. With their backs against the wall, the people cried out in fear. But Moses' faith in God was firm.

And Moses said to the people, "Fear not, stand firm, and see the salvation of the Lord, which he will work for you today; for the Egyptians whom you see today, you shall never see again. The Lord will fight for you, and you have only to be still."

Exodus 14:13-14

Upon speaking these words, Moses extended his staff and parted the Red Sea. And the Israelites passed over the dry land to safety. Meanwhile, driven by their hardened hearts, the entire Egyptian army chased after the Israelites into the dry seabed. But the waters returned to fill the sea, and the Egyptians were swallowed up and drowned. We know this story well.

Later, Moses reminded the people of the importance of keeping God's commandments in appreciation for what God did for them. And even today, this remembrance is recited in the Shema, a prayer that serves as a centerpiece to Jewish belief. Part of the Shema is taken from the Book of Exodus.

"When your son asks you in time to come, 'What is the meaning of the testimonies and the statutes and the ordinances which the Lord our God has commanded you?' then you shall say to your son, 'We were Pharaoh's slaves in Egypt; and the Lord brought us out of Egypt with a mighty hand.

Exodus 6:20-21

After crossing the Red Sea, things didn't get much easier, to say the least. The people wandered in the wilderness for 40 more years. They faced hostile resistance, hunger, thirst, and deep uncertainty about the future. During that time, I'm sure Moses had many sleepless nights. He must have doubted himself many times. Plus, he had to deal with the people's complaints.

The Hebrews groaned to Moses about their hardship as they traveled to the Promised Land. They even complained that they were better off as slaves. Imagine being a leader, guided by God's hand, and hearing that kind of complaint – "I'd rather be a slave, beaten and whipped, than be guided by you."

Time after time, God would bail them out. He sent them food and water. He gave them victories over enemies. He guided them through the wilderness with a pillar of cloud by day and a pillar of fire by night. Still, the people complained bitterly. But that wasn't the worst of it, not even close.

One day, Moses went up to Mount Sinai to receive the Tablets of the Covenant Law (the "Ten Commandments"). He spent 40 days and nights up there without food or water. It was a monumental moment for all humankind as God's law was being codified and given to Moses. Meanwhile, what happened at the foot of the mountain? After all God's great works and wonders, did the people wait patiently and faithfully? Nope.

> *When the people saw that Moses delayed to come down from the mountain, the people gathered themselves together to Aaron, and said to him, "Up, make us gods, who shall go before us; as for this Moses, the man who brought us up out of the land of Egypt, we do not know what has become of him." So all the people took off the rings of gold which were in their ears, and brought them to Aaron. And he received the gold at their hand, and fashioned it with a graving tool, and made a molten calf; and they said, "These are your gods, O Israel, who brought you up out of the land of Egypt!"*
>
> Exodus 32:1,3-4

While Moses was receiving God's Word on the mountain top, the people grew impatient. They quickly forgot about what God had done for them. So, they threw a party – but not just any party. They fell over themselves, drunkenly worshiping a graven image – a golden calf. Even worse, they gave the image credit for freeing them from Egypt. In blasphemous revelry, the people insulted God. The calf was a man-made god, a statue that the people worshiped. One can only imagine the level of debauchery that took place at that moment. It was a betrayal of epic proportions.

The first commandment warns against idolatry. Do you see why this makes perfect sense? Because if we forget about the one true God and create our own gods, then anything goes. We do whatever we want. If we are the god-makers, then we make the rules too. Every atrocity is allowed when we worship false gods. Chaos and depravity are allowed and encouraged.

How much of this do we see in our world today? How many idols do we construct in modern times? It's the money, power, and privilege we extract while others pay the price. The most horrible sin you can think of is allowed by gods we create ourselves. Why? Because ego, pride, and vanity are the real drivers behind every false god. The golden calf represents a terrible transgression against God and against ourselves.

What does all this have to do with humility? In the face of such serious iniquity, God had all the reason in the world to wipe out the people. God even said that he would spare Moses and give the prophet command over a new nation – while the rest of Israel would be exterminated. And at that critical moment, Moses showed great humility and devoted leadership. Even though he was deeply disappointed at what the people had done, Moses appealed to God's goodness.

> *So Moses went back to the Lord and said, "Oh, what a great sin these people have committed! They have made themselves gods of gold. But now, please forgive their sin—but if not, then blot me out of the book you have written."*

Exodus 32:31-32

Imagine that! Moses told God, if you get rid of them, then get rid of all of us – including me. Moses had done nothing wrong. He gave his life, effort, and service to the people. He was obedient and trustworthy. But if they could not be forgiven, Moses didn't want to be spared either. He interceded for those that disrespected him. The prophet interceded for those who committed wicked acts against God.

Moses didn't place himself apart from others, even when they made serious mistakes. He could have saved himself, but instead he gave of himself and appealed to God for the good of others. The humble intercede for the righteous and sinners alike. They ask for God's mercy for everyone – even their enemies.

Moses's example of the dedicated, humble leader was a prelude to the world-saving sacrifice that Jesus made centuries later. Moses followed a Christ-like pattern. Nevertheless, the leader of the Israelites also had to face his own limitations, as we will see in the next chapter.

Chapter 10: Accepting limits

Imagine working all your life towards a goal where you offered your service without holding anything back. Your work placed you in situations of danger, humiliation, and even betrayal. Still, you gave your whole effort to get the job done. The responsibility felt crushing sometimes. But you did it to serve God and your community. Maybe some of you already live in this kind of reality. Do you carry a great responsibility for your family, work, community, or church?

Now imagine that when your entire life's work is about to reach its peak, you're told you won't live to see it. That's exactly what happened to Moses. After decades in the desert, when the Israelites were about to enter the Promised Land, God told Moses that he would not enter.

Some say the reason for this was due to Moses' disobedience. At one point in their desert journey, the Israelites arrived at Kadesh, in the Desert of Zin. It was a hot and miserable place, and there was no water to quench their thirst. Again, the people complained bitterly to Moses. So he went to God and asked for help. The Lord told him to speak to a rock and that it would produce water.

> *"Take the rod, and assemble the congregation, you and Aaron your brother, and tell the rock before their eyes to yield its water; so you shall bring water out of the rock for them; so you shall give drink to the congregation and their cattle."*

Numbers 20:8

However, instead of speaking to the rock, Moses struck it twice with his staff. And water came gushing out.

> *And Moses and Aaron gathered the assembly together before the rock, and he said to them, "Hear now, you rebels; shall we bring forth water for you out of this rock?" And Moses lifted up his hand and struck the rock with his rod twice; and water came forth abundantly, and the congregation drank, and their cattle.*
Numbers 20:10-11

Why did Moses strike the rock instead of speaking to it? Was he tired and annoyed? Was he distracted by the heat? Nobody knows for sure, but still, Moses disobeyed. It might seem like a minor infraction. Was striking the rock instead of speaking to it such a big deal? Did this mean that after 40+ years of loyal service and sacrifice, Moses could not enter the Promised Land? Why such a harsh punishment? Later, Moses even prayed to God and asked if he could enter anyway. And God said no.

Why was the penalty so stiff? Was it because Moses' brother, Aaron, was there when God gave the command? Maybe it would have been a bad example if there was no consequence for Moses' disobedience. Or maybe it's meant to illustrate to us how serious obedience is for someone in a position of influence and authority.

There's one more detail to consider here. It has to do with Moses's attitude. If you look closely at the verses above, Moses says, "shall *we* bring forth water". By using the word "we" it's as if Moses wants to take credit for the miracle. Remember the golden calf? Who delivered the people out of bondage? Who provides water from the rock? Moses or God?

Moses knew God intimately. The prophet knew how serious it was to obey God's commands. So Moses humbled himself. He accepted the decision that forbade his entrance into the land flowing with milk and honey. And here we encounter a profound message for all of us. No matter how important you might be to a group or cause, if things fall apart in your absence, then there's a problem. If it continuously depends on you, then your leadership isn't solid. Even Moses's part in the story of salvation was limited. The people could move forward without him.

Near the end of his life, Moses told the Israelites that he would not cross over to the Promised Land. But instead of feeling sorry for himself, he encouraged the people. He didn't get caught up in ambition. He didn't have to be convinced to let go of his authority. Moses did not become bitter. He fully accepted that his time was coming to an end. The faithful prophet, leader, and lawgiver – and true friend of God – knew that the Lord's plan was much bigger than anyone could imagine. So Moses said to his people:

Be strong and of good courage ... for it is the Lord your God who goes with you; he will not fail you or forsake you.

Deuteronomy 31:6

For Moses, it was always about his community – God's people. Even when they rebelled or acted horribly, Moses was on their side. It wasn't about him or his legacy or being able to enjoy the fruits of his efforts. He served faithfully for as long as his people and God needed him. And when his time was up, Moses quietly stepped aside into history.

What lesson does Moses's experience teach you about your boundaries? When a difficult limit is set on you, how do you react?

Chapter 11: Is it really true?

 W hat can we take home from Moses' story? And how does it apply to being in tune with God? If we look back on Moses's life, many complex and amazing events occurred. Unexpected challenges appeared. And Moses, in his humanity, made mistakes. He doubted. He felt frustration, anger, and fear. He even disobeyed sometimes. But during it all, he was always seeking God. But why? What was Moses's deeper motive?

In the Book of Exodus, chapter 33, we find a fascinating exchange between God and Moses. It's a dialogue between two old friends. Moses asks God to *"show me now thy ways, that I may know thee and find favor in thy sight."*

And the Lord replied, *"My Presence will go with you, and I will give you rest."* Then Moses insists again to have the presence of God go with the people, otherwise he doesn't want to move an inch forward. And God grants this request. Then, on top of it all, Moses asks for something truly astounding. Moses asks God,

"I pray thee, show me thy glory."

Exodus 33:18

It's as if Moses can't get enough of God. He wants more and more, even to the point of asking for something extraordinary. Moses asks to see the glory of God up close and personal. And God grants this request as he is pleased with Moses. But how? How did Moses end up seeing God's glory? Supposedly, if anyone sees God's full glory, it would kill them. The scriptures explain it this way.

> *And the Lord said, "Behold, there is a place by me where you shall stand upon the rock; and while my glory passes by I will put you in a cleft of the rock, and I will cover you with my hand until I have passed by; then I will take away my hand, and you shall see my back; but my face shall not be seen."*

Exodus 33:21-33

So Moses got to see a glimpse of God as he passed by. Even with all Moses's doubts and mistakes, his heart was always wanting more of the Lord. This leads us to my favorite spiritual definition of humility: a humble heart can't get enough of God.

Saint Augustine wrote, *"You have made us for yourself, O Lord, and our hearts are restless until they rest in You."* The truly humble heart recognizes this and opens itself wide open to let the Holy Spirit in. Like Moses, the humble heart continuously invites God's Spirit in to do his work. They always feel poor when it comes to needing God. This can be one interpretation of what Jesus referred to when he said, *"Blessed are the poor in spirit, for theirs is the kingdom of heaven"* (Matthew 5:3). Even Jesus described himself this way. He said, *"I am gentle and lowly in heart"* (Matthew 11:29).

When a special guest comes over to visit you, what do you do? You start to sweep and straighten things up, right? You wash the dishes and clean up the clutter. But the humble heart invites the Spirit to enter without cleaning up first. The humble have no problem showing their dirty laundry and cobwebs in the corners.

67

God said to Moses, *"I know you by name."* Of course, God knew Moses's name. He knows everything about everyone. He's God. So what does this really mean – to "know you by name"? Maybe it means that Moses opened himself up completely to God's Spirit. He didn't try to hide or mask anything. He let the Spirit inside without trying to look good. Moses was sincere and authentic before God. He fully trusted the Lord. And that's what made him humble. Jesus also opened himself up to God, his Father. Even though he had no sin, Jesus experienced temptation, sorrow, and doubt. He knew his poverty of spirit could only be satisfied by God.

You might be thinking, "I wish I could open up like that. But I don't know if I can. I'm afraid and embarrassed. I don't even know how to start." Many of us feel this way. But remember, God doesn't expect you to be perfect. Many people make the mistake of thinking they must be good first – and only then can they go to God. But the exact opposite is true. He loves you and wants to help you as you are.

Jesus came for the sick and the sinners, not for the so-called perfect or good (Mark 2:17). When you open up and let the Spirit in, he heals you and frees you from the things that hold you back. And this is the best way to enter into harmony with God.

This process goes beyond just your healing and freedom. There is another powerful truth we sometimes forget about. Who is the Spirit that lives in the children of God? He is the same Spirit that created the universe. He is the Spirit that enabled the Virgin Mary to conceive a Son. He is the same Spirit that resurrected Jesus. And if you let him in, the Holy Spirit breathes life into your virtues and talents. Then God can use you for his holy will and his purposes. And perhaps, this is the ultimate expression of humility.

You see, true humility doesn't mean being silent and low key. Jesus was a hugely public figure. And he was the perfect, humble instrument of God. He let God's grace be fully expressed in his words and actions. Being in sync with the Lord means being a finely tuned instrument in his hands. This result is beautiful music played by the Creator. It's a solid life testimony. It's humility. It's knowing yourself and knowing God. It's intercession. It's accepting your limitations. And if needed, you wage combat against the enemy to bring healing and freedom to others as you yourself have been healed and freed by the Spirit of the Lord.

DISCOVER HUMILITY

There are hidden places inside each one of us. Secret rooms and dark corners where you left an episode of your life unfinished.

Maybe you don't care. Maybe you don't want to remember. Some of these places are scary, others were left lingering. Things were left undone and unsaid.

Those hidden places wait for you. You know they do, because they return to haunt you time and again.

Maybe you feel like they might devour you. Maybe you think what could have been – what if?

Would it all have been better if you reacted differently? What then? Could you have avoided disaster or pain after all these years?

If you did things differently, your life would have been better. Or not? And at times, the pangs of guilt and shame overwhelm you.

You wonder, how you can live with yourself, with your story? It's an indelible stain. And no matter how hard you try to scrub it off, the wound rubs raw.

Since that time, you've grown. You've learned. Things have changed and so have you. Back then you were young, and you didn't know.

And your younger self looks up at you and says, it's true. I didn't understand. If I only knew. If I only understood. And the depths of your heart ache to see you back then.

And the Lord tells you, that's the place. That's the place where I wish to go. If you let me. If you trust. For I am gentle and lowly in heart.

And the Lord of all creation himself will enter that place. Gently. Tenderly. It is a sacred place. It's that corner of your heart where nobody's allowed in.

Yet from there, so much fear, anger, and confusion pour out. You might not even realize it, but the undertow carries the force of a thousand horses.

And against that powerful river of pain, the Lord fights relentlessly to reach you. He will not rest until he rescues you.

Standing in front of the door is the accuser, the tempter. He blocks the way. The evil one says to the Lord, you will not enter here.

You see, the devil says, this part is mine. This part I keep locked up at all times. Here is where I keep my prisoner, my slave.

And the Lord looks past the tempter. He sees you behind the door, frozen, fearful yet wanting, hoping. And he waits for one word.

He asks you, can I come in? Will you let me in to set you free again, to take you home?

And if needed, the Lord waits for you for years, decades even, a lifetime. He waits until he hears that one word.

Yes.

Yes, Lord. Save me. Set me free.

And at that very instant the accuser vanishes. His substance amounts to nothing against the unleashed mercy of God.

And the Lord Jesus comes to you. He takes you out of the corner. He frees you from the hidden room. He takes you by the hand.

He loves you, but not with a distant, abstract love.

Jesus Christ loves you with a human heart.

So stand up. Step forth, O child of God. You were created to be loved.

Return to God's original plan for you. Embrace life here, now, even though you've walked upon a thorny path. Even though you've been hurt and shamed.

But our Lord is never ashamed of you. Never, ever, not in a million years. His heart bleeds for you. And the blood of the Lamb cleanses your wounds.

No more hiding. No more secret rooms. Only the spacious love of God remains.

So go. Roam free, O child of God.

The Spirit gives you new wings to soar high. This is your new life.

Taste the everlasting sweetness for your soul.

> *"Come to me, all who labor and are heavy laden, and I will give you rest. Take my yoke upon you, and learn from me; for I am gentle and lowly in heart, and you will find rest for your souls. For my yoke is easy, and my burden is light."*

Matthew 11:28-30

Chapter 12: Suddenly, all seems lost

When you first think about living in tune with God's Spirit, it sounds wonderful. I mean, who wouldn't want to be in sync with the Creator of the universe? Everything in your life should flow nicely then, right? We all know, however, life is unpredictable. Situations change all the time. But what happens when things go wildly off-course?

We're all familiar with the scene. Everything seems to be fine in your life or at least relatively stable – then, BANG! A crisis explodes in your face. It might be an issue with a loved one. It could be an illness, accident, financial strife, drug abuse, betrayal, or a nasty fight. Now, I'm not talking about a minor bump in the road. I'm talking about major events that shake you to your core. Is it possible to remain in synchrony with God even in moments of extreme difficulty?

Believe it or not, as I write this, I'm going through a rough moment in my life. The events surrounding Omar have quieted down considerably. Ruben is mourning the loss of his brother, but he is at peace. I went to visit Omar in the hospital during his last days. As he drifted in and out of consciousness, he looked at me and shook my hand.

At one point, I leaned in close to him. I whispered into his ear. I said, "Omar, you know you have been wounded. You know you have made mistakes. But know this: God loves you. He sent his Son to forgive you and to take you with him to paradise. Accept the forgiveness of the Lord. Do not be afraid Omar. Do not be afraid of God's love." And as I continued to pray and whisper in Omar's ear, he eventually fell asleep. I'm not sure how much he understood, but the "good thief" that was crucified with Jesus gives me great hope.

> *Two others also, who were criminals, were led away to be put to death with him. And when they came to the place which is called The Skull, there they crucified him, and the criminals, one on the right and one on the left.*

> Luke 23:32-33

God gives us free will to choose. We are free to reject him, even with the last breath of our lives. If people reject love during their entire life, I believe they can also reject love at the moment of their death.

Some people get angry at the notion of hell. They think, how could God allow such a place to exist? The reason is that God gives us free will. It may be the greatest power we possess. Free will lets us choose between life and death. We can even choose hell if we want to. You might ask, who would choose that?

Think about it. How many opt for a hellish existence every day? How many choose corruption and lies? How many push away and betray those that love them? How many step on others to get ahead? How many sell drugs, exploit children, and make a fortune from weapons of war? I know, in my past, I chose things that weren't good for me. I chose evil. At the time, the choices I made condemned me.

And this is the judgment, that the light has come into the world, and men loved darkness rather than light, because their deeds were evil. For every one who does evil hates the light, and does not come to the light, lest his deeds should be exposed.

John 3:19-20

My hope is that Omar had an encounter with Jesus, accepted his forgiveness, and went to heaven. At any life ending moment, I believe God can appear, stop time, and give each soul a last chance at salvation. In the end, he always lets us choose. Perhaps it's a naïve way to see things. It's simple hope and trust in God's mercy. The "good thief" who was crucified with Jesus shows us how this can happen.

One of the criminals who hung there hurled insults at him: "Aren't you the Messiah? Save yourself and us!"

But the other criminal rebuked him. "Don't you fear God," he said, "since you are under the same sentence? We are punished justly, for we are getting what our deeds deserve. But this man has done nothing wrong."

Then he said, "Jesus, remember me when you come into your kingdom."

Jesus answered him, "Truly I tell you, today you will be with me in paradise."

Luke 23:39-43

Omar died the next day. Did he go to heaven? Only God knows. But one thing is for sure, Jesus gives you a chance to be with him even until the last breath of your life. And that gives me great hope.

Now, what about when things get out of control? What does all this have to do with crisis situations? Right now, I'm facing a very hard personal struggle. The situation involves someone very close to me. I pray we might learn together how to navigate these moments.

Earlier today, I was praying to God, and I was crying. Honestly, I don't cry easily, but the pain I felt this morning drove deep. It was a combination of shame, worry, sadness, and anguish. What happened to being in sync with God? Can someone who is walking with the Lord feel this way? I know Jesus did (except for shame). When he prayed in the garden of Gethsemane – on the eve of his crucifixion – Jesus felt deep anguish. I imagine the universe itself must have shuddered when the Son of God knelt in prayer the night before he faced his trial and crucifixion.

In 2 Corinthians it says, *"God made him who had no sin to be sin for us, so that in him we might become the righteousness of God."* That's a difficult thing to think about, isn't it? Jesus became sin. So maybe even Jesus did feel something like shame. Could there have been anything worse for Jesus than to become sin in front of his Father? Think about being condemned for a crime even though you are innocent. Could there be anything more humiliating?

Right now, I'm facing an ongoing issue with a loved one, and the problem seems to be getting worse. I know he's in danger. He does not want to see it or admit it. In fact, he even flaunts his dangerous behavior. Just writing these words brings back a tightness in my chest and a sense of sadness mixed with anxiety.

And the questions come flooding in. Why Lord? Where did things go wrong? Is it my fault? How is my loved one's conduct going to influence others? Should I say something? How? When? How will all this impact my loved one's future? How do I handle watching someone I care about put their life and health at risk? And yes, I admit it; I feel ashamed. And maybe that's selfish since it's about my loved one, not me. And even as I write these words, I feel like crying again.

So I keep telling myself that everyone has a cross to carry. I say to myself that things will get better. I tell myself to keep praying hard. God's word reminds me over and over again to trust in his promises. But it still hurts. It stings. And there's a knot in my throat and a heaviness in my heart that won't go away for a while. What do you do when someone you love hurts themselves?

My prayers the last few days have been intense. They move back and forth from tears to anger and to anguish. I even found myself punching my pillow to release my frustration and rage. Is this the image of a man in harmony with God? I even thought to myself at one point, "Who in the world do you think you are writing a book about being in sync with God? Just look at yourself. What a joke."

Later, my thoughts turned to Job, a man whom the scriptures say was blameless and upright. Job feared God and shunned evil. But terrible things happened to him, and he lost everything he had. Then Job's children were tragically killed when a roof collapsed on them.

And I think of the parable of the Merciful Father (some call it the parable of the Prodigal Son). The father in the parable represents God our Father. Even though the father in the parable was merciful and kind, his son left him to squander his inheritance and live a licentious life. Was it the father's fault?

And then I think of Jesus, who chose Judas as one of his disciples. This choice led to the worst betrayal in all of history. And Judas ended up killing himself. Did Jesus make a mistake? Why didn't his Father warn him?

No, I am not blameless like Job. I'm not a father like the one in the parable either. And I'm certainly not Jesus. Tremendous trials happened to these people. Many good people have faced incredibly tough situations. And some even faced deep humiliation. Why should I think it can't happen to me? Even though I try to be in tune with the Lord, does it mean I will never face painful moments?

Remember when I mentioned I struggle with humility? Maybe this is an opportunity to get better in that aspect of my life. It's not that God sends me problems to force me to be humble, but in his spiritual economy, nothing goes to waste. What do you think? Do you agree that trials make you humbler?

In the end, Job was restored. He regained all his goods and had even more children. The prodigal son came home, and the father threw a big party as his son returned to life. And Jesus, well you know. He rose again on the third day. He saved the world from sin and death. And the thief that was crucified with Jesus? He asked Jesus to remember him and was taken directly to paradise.

Even in the darkest moments, we can be in harmony with the Lord. Even when your world appears to be falling apart, the true love of Christ cannot be denied or diluted. And if you hold on tight to him, you can remain faithful despite the pain.

These critical moments may take shape after a long time. They might be the result of bad decisions you made years ago. No matter what, we all stumble through life trying to find our way. We can be hardheaded or blind. We can also be misguided. Nobody has all the answers up front, and some lessons take a long time to learn.

Eventually, the truth is revealed to you, and it can manifest itself in a crisis. Many times, it happens on a personal or relationship level. Don't be mistaken though. A crisis can occur without any direct correlation to your past. It's not always your fault. It might not be about who's to blame at all, but rather unfortunate circumstances. In so many cases, we are all victims and all sinners at once. But during it all, if you listen, deep truths are revealed to you.

During those darkest moments, when the pain is so great, some come to identify with the crucified One in the most intimate way. Only those that suffer deeply can know something of the suffering of Christ. This might not be much of a consolation. Nobody seeks this voluntarily – but it is a great spiritual truth.

When all your pride, fear, and hesitation have subsided, you become more like Jesus. You reach a point where all you can do is trust the Father and abandon yourself to his sacred will.

Remember, nobody is ever forced to go to hell. God does everything he can to convince you to embrace heaven. He holds nothing back, not even the life of his beloved Son. The promise of paradise is for everyone and anyone who truly wants it. No mistake is too big. And as long as you live and breathe, it's never too late. But this is not a message about death. Instead, it's a great hope for life. It's a living hope that sustains you even during the hardest times.

So please, O Lord, do not forget about my loved one. Do not forget about me. **I appeal to your loving goodness**, as that's about all I have right now.

> *Who shall separate us from the love of Christ? Shall tribulation, or distress, or persecution, or famine, or nakedness, or peril, or sword? As it is written,*
> *"For thy sake we are being killed all the day long;*
> *we are regarded as sheep to be slaughtered."*
> *No, in all these things we are more than conquerors through him who loved us. For I am sure that neither death, nor life, nor angels, nor principalities, nor things present, nor things to come, nor powers, nor height, nor depth, nor anything else in all creation, will be able to separate us from the love of God in Christ Jesus our Lord.*

Romans 8:35-39

Chapter 13: Going out to sea

In every crisis, there's an opportunity. Even though we don't enjoy hard trials, they provide us with a chance to grow. Hard times teach you to be patient. A deep crisis shows you how to cling tighter to God. Wisdom may only come after you've been banged up a bit, and the truly wise have the scars to show for it. But could there be other hidden meanings behind difficult life experiences? Could God be trying to reveal something more to you?

Every chapter you've read up to now was written several months ago. I wasn't sure if I would ever publish this book. When I started, the book seemed like a good idea, but then it sat there on the shelf, waiting. So from here forward, we enter a spiritual laboratory. Let's hope God's Spirit speaks to us to give nourishment to our souls. Let's venture into deeper waters.

Believe it or not, the crisis I described in the last chapter was nothing compared to a new crisis I recently experienced. I couldn't believe it, but the first one was just a warm up. Again, I'm not Job, but in my own small way, I experienced something like he did. How do you react when one tragedy after another appears in rapid succession?

In Job's case, he received a sudden visit from his servant messenger (Job 1:13-19). It was terrible news. A neighboring tribe, the Sabeans, had attacked and stolen Job's oxen and donkeys. The attackers also killed his servants. Job's servant hadn't even finished speaking when another messenger appeared saying *"The fire of God fell from the heavens and burned up the sheep and the servants, and I am the only one who has escaped to tell you!"*

While he was still speaking, a third messenger appeared and said, *"The Chaldeans formed three raiding parties and swept down on your camels and made off with them. They put the servants to the sword, and I am the only one who has escaped to tell you!"*

While he was still speaking, yet another messenger appeared with the worst news of all. He said, *"Your sons and daughters were feasting and drinking wine at the oldest brother's house, when suddenly a mighty wind swept in from the desert and struck the four corners of the house. It collapsed on them and they are dead, and I am the only one who has escaped to tell you!"*

Within the span of minutes, Job received news that he had lost his livestock, camels, servants, and, worst of all, his children. Who can possibly recover from so much bad news? It would be the greatest understatement of all time to say this was a life-changing moment for Job. And his initial reaction to these events astounds me.

At this, Job got up and tore his robe and shaved his head. Then he fell to the ground in worship and said:

"Naked I came from my mother's womb,
  and naked I will depart.
The Lord gave and the Lord has taken away;
  may the name of the Lord be praised."
In all this, Job did not sin by charging God with wrongdoing.

Job 1:20-22

After receiving such terrible news, Job worshiped God. Incredible!

80

Recently, I lived through a Job-like experience, but on a much smaller scale. In my case, a person was killed, my income shrank to a trickle, and bills came due that were five times what I expected. Also, the lives of some people close to me began to fall apart at the seams. By giving this short summary, I don't mean to minimize the seriousness of these events. I can't give all the details, but I can say the events were deeply painful and tragic.

When many major crises hit you all at once, how do you manage? All this happened to me within a week or so. No, it's not a Job-level tragedy, not even close. But for me, I can say it was one of the most difficult times in my life. I'm sure you've faced similar situations.

Yes, Job fell down and worshiped God when the bad news hit, but later things got even worse for him. He was stricken with *"painful sores from the soles of his feet to the crown of his head"*. Then his wife cursed God and resented Job's integrity. And eventually, Job too became bitter. He began to feel that his life was meaningless and worthless. And in his bitterness, Job cried out to God:

> *If I have sinned, what have I done to you, you who see everything we do?*
> *Why have you made me your target? Have I become a burden to you?*
> *"Why then did you bring me out of the womb? I wish I had died before any eye saw me.*
> *If only I had never come into being, or had been carried straight from the womb to the grave!*

Job 7:20, 10:18-19

Even though my situation wasn't nearly as bad, I understand how Job felt. When you go through a major crisis, especially when many things go wrong at once, you might look up to heaven and say, "Are you kidding me? How much more do you think I can take?" You might fall into a state of anguish. You might even have thoughts about worthlessness or death like Job did.

When I visit the prison, one question comes up repeatedly. Why do innocent people suffer? Why do good people get hurt or die? And these questions come up for a good reason. Nearly all of those in jail suffered some kind of injustice when they were young and vulnerable.

Some people say it's due to sin. Once sin got into the world, they say, bad things began to happen, even unimaginable evil. Others say unfortunate events always lead to greater good. When something bad happens, something good comes out of it later.

Also, God loves us and gives us free will. We are free to choose, even things that hurt ourselves and others. Meanwhile, God lets bad things happen so we can choose to make things better.

These are all reasonable explanations, and we'll continue to explore them later. Still, they might not give much comfort to the mother who lost her child due to cancer. They might not bring much comfort to victims of mental or physical abuse. For those who live in the slums of Calcutta, these quick answers can't soothe the pain or ease the hunger. In Job's case, his bitterness deepened, and he fell into a pit of despair.

> *I cry out to you, God, but you do not answer; I stand up, but you merely look at me.*
>
> *You turn on me ruthlessly; with the might of your hand you attack me.*
>
> *Yet when I hoped for good, evil came; when I looked for light, then came darkness.*
>
> *The churning inside me never stops; days of suffering confront me.*

Job 30:20-21, 26-27

During more than 30 chapters in the book, Job and his friends debate over the question that has puzzled and challenged humankind forever: why do good people suffer? Eventually, God gave Job an answer:

> *"Where were you when I laid the earth's foundation?*
> *Tell me, if you understand.*
> *Who marked off its dimensions? Surely you know!*
> *Do you know the laws of the heavens?*
> *Can you set up God's dominion over the earth?*

Job 38:4-5,33

From there the Lord describes his dominion over all creation – the earth, the heavens, the stars, and planets. He challenges Job to explain how God keeps all living creatures alive and how earth's wondrous cycles are established.

It's as if God said, "Listen. You can complain all you want about how human life and the universe work. You can shake your fist and curse me all you like. But that won't change anything. How can you expect God to explain to you how all existence works and comes together?"

How do some of us react to this? When this is God's answer to our worst tragedies, how do we respond? Some remain bitter and resentful. Others decide to not believe in God anymore. Some stay angry at him during their entire lives. In the face of great pain, these reactions are all understandable, but none of them give you closure. None of them bring comfort to the soul. None of them gives you peace.

One of God's most powerful responses to Job's bitterness was this:

> *"Would you discredit my justice?*
> *Would you condemn me to justify yourself?"*

Job 40:8

And eventually Job replied,

83

Surely I spoke of things I did not understand,
* things too wonderful for me to know.*
"You said, 'Listen now, and I will speak;
* I will question you,*
* and you shall answer me.'*
My ears had heard of you
* but now my eyes have seen you.*
Therefore I despise myself
* and repent in dust and ashes."*

Job 42:3-6

Job's words are powerful. Now, God does not want us to despise ourselves, but he does want us to live in truth. He does want us to be able to move past our pain. When you experience loss or hurt, it's natural to feel strong emotions. You can get angry, even at God. Job was blameless and upright, but he also complained bitterly to God. We all need time to process the hardest moments, and we should take all the time we need.

But if we remain in sorrow and despair for too long, what happens? Inevitably, hurt and pain become the center of our existence. Our hurt grows into unreasonable proportions. All we're left with is pain, and these things become our gods. If sadness and bitterness occupy the core of your being, then it impacts everything. Eventually, to move forward, you come to a point where you must choose life again, no matter how much it hurts.

Now all of this might make sense to the head, but what about the heart? Sure, we can try to reason our way out of the tragedy of life. But for the weary, damaged soul, does any of this bring closure? Sometimes, even for the hardest questions in life, we want neat and tidy answers. It's our nature to seek easy explanations. But the hardest life experiences require something more than a one-line response. Words alone aren't enough.

So, what is God's answer to all the suffering, sin, and pain in the world? There can only be one answer. Let's find out what it is.

Chapter 14: A long way to go

When times get tough, I mean life-changing level tough, you can choose from several options. You can decide to shut down. You can fight your way out, or you can run away. Or you can lean deeper into your faith. The last option might be the most challenging because it means you must trust. You must believe. And it's never easy when you face many battle fronts at once.

If we want to gain the full understanding of our humanity, including suffering, we must follow the path of the Messiah. But to do this, to move closer into sync with the Lord, sometimes things get shaken up a bit.

As I mentioned earlier, I recently faced a Job-like experience which helped me understand things about myself which is essential to be more in tune with God. It started a few months ago when my family and I went on vacation. Things were going great. Work was good, and the kids were healthy. The trip was fantastic, and everybody was getting along superbly.

I rejoiced in prayer each morning and watched the sun rise over the rugged hills of the Sierra Chica in the province of Cordoba. The low mountain angles of brown and green invited me to explore each crevasse while a flock of sheep bleated to greet the sun. I was at peace. I was thankful for my life.

Then suddenly, tragedy turned my world upside down. We received a call one night about a tragic event that happened to a loved one who's far from home. Someone (not my loved one) had been killed. It was devastating news. When things like this happen, your mind bounces around from numb disbelief to seeking blame to deep anguish. So we ended our vacation and made the long drive home worrying about how things would turn out.

While still reeling from the news, I received an email upon returning home. One of my clients, who provides 99% of my income, told me they wouldn't be needing my writing services anymore. Then I received a surprise notice from my son's school telling me his next tuition payment would be five times higher than before. My income had dropped to near-zero, and now I had a huge bill to pay. And when I went searching for new clients, the search had become 20 times harder compared to a few years ago.

At the same time, a close friend's family began to fall apart, and he fell back into drug abuse. Meanwhile, another friend of mine had gone broke, and he asked me for money so he could eat. Argentina has the third highest rate of inflation in the world right now. About 50% of the population lives in poverty. It seems like every other day someone comes knocking on the door asking for a handout. Times are tough here.

Needless to say, I was deeply disturbed by all these events. The pressure was intense. And the ugly face of the accuser appeared again, to taunt me, "So this is what it looks like to be in tune with God? You are a fool."

Then, as I scrambled to find new clients, allocate my tight finances, and support my loved one, the Spirit called me. What did he say? What could he possibly say to me when I felt like my life was falling apart?

The Spirit told me this: lean deeper into prayer and God's Word.

Wait. What? How? Of course, I know all about the importance of acceptance. I'm aware that I should stay hopeful and that things will get better. And I know God has a purpose for everything, good and bad. But I was worried sick about my loved one. My economy was in shambles. People's lives around me were getting torn to pieces. I had never faced anything like this before. But the Spirit called to me again.

Get to know Elijah, he told me. Study his story. What might this prophet have to teach us about facing extremely hard moments in life?

With a constant knot in my stomach, it took all my might to dig into prayer. At night, I typically like to wind down and watch sports or the news. Now I was called to get to know the prophet Elijah. I was called to prayer.

Elijah is one of the greatest prophets in the Old Testament, and he's mentioned frequently in the New Testament too. During Elijah's time, Ahab was king of Israel, and Jezebel was Ahab's queen. King Ahab wasn't the best leader of his time. In fact, he was a disaster. He built an altar and a temple dedicated to the pagan deity Baal, and this offended God greatly. In the book of 1 Kings, it says Ahab *"did more to arouse the anger of the Lord, the God of Israel, than did all the kings of Israel before him."* In this context of great offense to God, the prophet Elijah declared that a severe drought would bring affliction to the land.

> *"As the Lord the God of Israel lives, before whom I stand, there shall be neither dew nor rain these years, except by my word."*
>
> 1 Kings 17:1

Later, Elijah experienced and performed several miracles. During the drought, while he hid by the brook Cherith, some ravens delivered bread and meat to him. Elijah then produced a never-ending supply of flour and oil for a starving widow and her son. And the prophet even revived the widow's son back to life from the dead.

By far the most famous episode in Elijah's history, however, was his victory over the 450 prophets of Baal on Mount Carmel. King Ahab and his wife Jezebel used these prophets to spread a religion that was in direct conflict with the God of Israel.

As a staunch defender of the faith in the one true God, Elijah challenged the prophets to a contest. He set up the contest like this: each side – the prophets of Baal vs. Elijah – had to place a bull, cut into pieces, onto an altar of wood for a fire. Then, whoever's god brought down fire to burn up their bull offering would be declared the winner.

> *"And you call on the name of your god and I will call on the name of the Lord; and the God who answers by fire, he is God." And all the people answered, "It is well spoken."*

1 Kings 18:24

Dancing around the bull on the altar they had built, the prophets of Baal cried out to their god from morning until noon. But nothing happened. Elijah mocked them saying that maybe their god was distracted or sleeping. The prophets continued in a frenzy, cutting themselves with swords and lances. Their blood gushed out while they continued to call out to Baal, but no one answered.

Then it was Elijah's turn. He built up his altar with 12 stones to represent the 12 tribes of Israel. Then he dug a large trench around the altar and had the people douse the bull offering, the wood, and the altar with water three times. Everything was soaked, and even the trench was filled with water as well.

Then the prophet Elijah stepped forward and prayed:

> *"Lord, the God of Abraham, Isaac, and Israel, let it be known today that you are God in Israel and that I am your servant and have done all these things at your command.*

Answer me, Lord, answer me, so these people will know that you, Lord, are God, and that you are turning their hearts back again."

Then the fire of the Lord fell from heaven. It burned up the sacrifice, the wood, the stones, and the soil. The fire of the Lord dried up the water in the trench. When the people saw this, they fell to the ground and cried out, *"The Lord—he is God! The Lord—he is God!"* And the prophets of Baal were seized and killed. It was an epic victory for God's prophet (1 Kings 18:20-46). Later, Elijah called for an end to the drought.

If you've been walking in faith for some time, you might feel a bit like Elijah. The Lord may have won some great victories in your life. I know he has for me. He helped me leave behind many toxic behaviors. He showed me how to repair relationships. And he's used me to help spread his Good News to places like prisons. My marriage is healthy and strong, and I'm part of a united community of faith in our parish.

I am far from perfect. I still sin. I struggle with vanity and pride. But I can't deny the work the Holy Spirit has done in my life. It's all due to the goodness of the Lord, and I'm thankful. Maybe you've received similar blessings. But how solid is our faith when the sky darkens and the thunder, lightning, and heavy rain appear?

After Elijah's awesome victory over the 450 prophets, something curious happened. We know that the 450 prophets were under the control of Jezebel, King Ahab's wife. She was the real motor behind the activity of the prophets of Baal. When she heard the news of her team's defeat, she was furious. And she threatened to kill Elijah.

So Jezebel sent a messenger to Elijah to say, "May the gods deal with me, be it ever so severely, if by this time tomorrow I do not make your life like that of one of them." Elijah was afraid and ran for his life.

1 Kings 19:2-3

Here we have God's prophet, his heavy hitter, who single handedly dismantled the 450 prophets of Baal. But the threat of just one woman filled him with intense fear. It says Elijah *"ran for his life."* What caused this reaction? Why did this larger-than-life prophet and miracle worker suddenly turn tail and run?

We find the answer in the person who threatened him – Jezebel. She zealously promoted false gods. Jezebel was the daughter of Ethbaal, king of the Sidonians. And judging from his name which means "toward the idol" or "with Baal", Ethbaal was likely a high priest of Baal. And who is Baal? He is one of Satan's chief demons. And I believe that's what filled the great prophet Elijah with fear. He knew a powerful demonic force was behind Jezebel's threat.

So there I was, facing my own multi-headed crisis – sudden tragedy, no income, few work opportunities, friends' lives falling apart – all occurring at once. And I too was filled with fear. Was a demonic spirit behind the events surrounding me? Or was it all just coincidence? I can't be certain, but I can say darkness fell around me and tried to tear me apart. And in that context, I was led to follow the story of Elijah.

During the crisis, I felt as if I was alone in the wilderness. But as the Spirit guided me, I leaned harder into my faith. It was not easy, but I poured and prayed over the Word telling me Elijah's story. At one truly dark moment, I was tempted to give up all hope. I can't remember the last time I experienced such darkness in my heart before.

Then I came upon the part in scripture where Elijah fell down exhausted. He collapsed under a tree, and said, *"It is enough; now, O Lord, take away my life; for I am no better than my fathers."* And then Elijah fell asleep.

I totally identified with Elijah's exhaustion. When you are pushed to your limit in multiple areas, you sometimes just want to collapse. But things didn't end there for Elijah and not for me either.

The scriptures say that an angel appeared to Elijah and touched him. The angel said to him, *"Arise and eat."* And Elijah looked and saw a cake baked on hot stones and a jar of water. So he ate and drank, and he laid down again. Then the angel of the Lord came a second time, touched him again, and said, *"Arise and eat, else the journey will be too great for you."* And Elijah arose, ate, and drank. Now strengthened, the prophet journeyed forty days and forty nights to Horeb, the mount of God (1 Kings 19:3-9).

As I read this passage, it spoke to me at the most profound level. I too felt weak and exhausted by worry and fear. But as I fed on God's Word, it was as if I was nibbling on the crumbs of the cake left by the angel. Even though my situation had not changed at all, I regained a tiny bit of strength, a whisper of hope.

Are you facing a tough situation right now? Are you tempted to give up hope sometimes? Listen to God's word when he says to you, *"Yes child. I know this is a hard time for you. But get up, arise! This is not the last chapter in your life. You still have a long way to go. ARISE!"*

Chapter 15: The night in the cave

It was excruciating. Like I said, my crisis moment was one of the most difficult times of my life. Still, it can't compare to other stories, not even close. The testimonies of some believers humble you to a major degree.

Take Immaculée Ilibagiza, for example. Her story is beyond incredible. She grew up as a happy and carefree child in Rwanda. She went to school and enjoyed her life among friends and her close-knit family. Her future was full of promise. Then suddenly, events in her country took a horrific turn.

In the Rwandan Civil War of 1994, Immaculée's life was changed forever. During the brutal conflict, a genocide took place where up to 1 million people were killed during a 100-day period. Immaculée's mother, father, and two brothers were all killed by soldiers. At one point she was forced to hide for three months in a tiny bathroom with seven other women to escape death. It was an extremely bloody conflict rife with atrocities of all kinds, and Immaculée lived through it to tell her story.

Even though my troubles weren't even close to what Immaculée experienced, I don't have to compare myself to her.

And neither does anyone else. When you are living through a critical moment, one of the worst things you might hear is something like, "Well at least you're not dying from hunger" or something like that. Yes, it could always be much worse, but that doesn't mean you don't worry. It doesn't mean you don't hurt. Every serious trial impacts us in a strong way.

When you go through a major crisis, a meeting with God will eventually take place. Immaculée had intense encounters with God during those long weeks in hiding. Sometimes soldiers came into the house and searched for the women. She could hear their shouting and cursing, and she felt the violence in their voices. The women could have been discovered at any moment, and their fate would have been unimaginable. Immaculée prayed and wrestled with her faith many times during those long months in hiding.

And the prophet Elijah? What did he do after being threatened by Jezebel, the daughter of Ethbaal, the high priest of the demon Baal? Elijah struggled intensely with his fear too. How do we know this? The scriptures tell us he sat down under a tree and wished for death. But then an angel touched him. And the Lord gently nursed him back to life.

From there, Elijah wandered for 40 days in the wilderness until he reached Mount Horeb. There, the prophet entered a cave to spend the night. That evening a voice appeared and said to him, *"What are you doing here, Elijah?"* And at that point, the prophet released all his frustration and anxiety. Elijah laid it all out at God's feet. He presented his impossible situation to the Lord.

> *He replied, "I have been very zealous for the Lord God Almighty. The Israelites have rejected your covenant, torn down your altars, and put your prophets to death with the sword. I am the only one left, and now they are trying to kill me too."*

> 1 Kings 19:13-14

Who hasn't spent a night in that cave? Who hasn't faced a sleepless night worrying about a lost or sick loved one? Who hasn't worried about money problems? Who hasn't tossed and turned due to mistakes you made or a conflict with someone? You roll the problem around in your head a thousand times. It's like trying to solve a Rubik's cube with hundreds of sides and colors. You look at it from every angle – above, below, left, and right – but you can't solve it no matter how hard you try. Still, like Elijah's night in the cave, in every crisis, there's a chance to encounter God.

> *Then a great and powerful wind tore the mountains apart and shattered the rocks before the Lord, but the Lord was not in the wind. After the wind there was an earthquake, but the Lord was not in the earthquake. After the earthquake came a fire, but the Lord was not in the fire. And after the fire came a gentle whisper.*
> *When Elijah heard it, he pulled his cloak over his face and went out and stood at the mouth of the cave.*
>
> 1 Kings 19:11-13

During the hard trials and sleepless nights, it happens exactly like that sometimes, doesn't it? The wailing wind, earthquakes, fire, and shattering rocks – you struggle with yourself when you face something grim. But then, if you give him space, if you pay attention, God shows up. When the dust settles, the Lord speaks in the gentle breeze.

The gesture of Elijah pulling his cloak over his face at that point fascinates me. After the gentle whisper of God, Elijah hides his face. Within the narrative it's just a few short words, but they hold so much meaning. Why did Elijah cover his face when God's Spirit whispered to him? He didn't cover his face during the fierce wind, earthquake, or fire. But in the gentle breeze, in the presence of God, Elijah covered his face.

I believe this was Elijah expressing his fear of God – but not the same type of fear he felt from Jezebel's threats. Instead, it's the feeling of profound respect and awe in the presence of the Creator. It's knowing there's so much more space for you to grow when you walk with the Lord.

Moses also hid his face when he met God for the first time in the burning bush on Mount Sinai. Even Jesus fell on his face, covering it when he prayed in the garden of Gethsemane, the night before his death. You cover your face when the greatness of God reveals a difficult, but all important, purpose for your life.

Then God asked Elijah for a second time, *"What are you doing here, Elijah?"* At that point, the prophet repeated the exact same story to God. Nothing had changed on the outside, but a process was unfolding inside Elijah.

He replied, *"I have been very zealous for the Lord God Almighty. The Israelites have rejected your covenant, torn down your altars, and put your prophets to death with the sword. I am the only one left, and now they are trying to kill me too."* (1 Kings 19:14).

After the turbulent night, in the presence of the Lord, you eventually find peace. You might be called to prayer in the middle of the night. Or God's peace may come with sleep or after the dawn. He shows you how things come together. He helps you solve the complex riddles in your mind. But there's something else going on here – something much deeper and more profound if you are willing to reach for it.

If you were paying attention, in the last chapter, I mentioned that "At night, I typically like to wind down and watch sports or the news." You probably just skimmed over it, hardly even noticing. But here's the thing. Sometimes I might spend an hour or two (or more?) at night with my cell phone. And the time that I protect as "me time" is sometimes just empty watching.

Yes, we all need to zone out once in a while, but I can overdo it at times. And God doesn't want us to be digital zombies. Maybe Elijah's mistake was when he ridiculed the 450 prophets of Baal.

Maybe during the contest, Elijah overdid it and called too much attention to himself.

God wants us to be free of pettiness and live full of purpose and integrity. He wants us to know we only get one shot at life, and we should value every second as if it's our last. But there's even more. What he wants, what God really wants, is your heart. And he wants all of it.

Remember Elijah's prayer when he called down God's fire from the sky during the contest against the 450 prophets of Baal? Elijah prayed, *"So these people will know that you, Lord, are God, and that you are turning their hearts back again."*

Although tough times aren't meant to expose your weakness, it can happen. Again, in God's economy, nothing goes to waste. In my case, the earthquake shook out some things that were hurting my growth. The Lord showed me my "me time" rituals were sometimes wasteful, not restful. Maybe Elijah had to learn to be humbler to serve God better.

During my night in the cave, I collapsed to my knees in prayer. I felt deep anguish due to my multi-headed crisis. I was shaken to the core of my being. The wind howled all around me. Even though my trials can't compare, it was as if I was in the cave with Elijah. I was in that bathroom during the genocide with Immaculée, intensely worried.

As the hurricane, earthquake, and raging fire calmed down, I cried out for God's help and mercy. I wasn't zoning out watching videos. I wasn't wasting time on my phone. Instead, I was praying. I was reading my Bible. In my pain and fear, I reached out to God. I was in communion with my Creator. And at that moment, he had all my heart.

But isn't that what we all really want deep down? Isn't that what my wife and kids want from me? They want all my heart. Isn't that what we truly want from the ones we love? And the Lord gives you all his heart as well. Nobody loves you more than Jesus – with all his human heart.

There's one more detail to consider in the richness of Elijah's story. And you don't want to miss this. It's the key to everything from here forward. This is the cornerstone for being in sync with God, the Creator of heaven and earth.

Where did Elijah go after he was revived by the angel who left him cakes and water? Where did he witness the wind, quakes, and fire? Where did Elijah receive the gentle breeze of the Holy Spirit? It was on Mount Horeb (also called Mount Sinai). What happened on that mountain long before Elijah climbed up there?

On Mount Horeb the Lord gave Moses the Law of the Covenant. It was on that mountain that a sacred alliance between God and humans was established. And in the deepest alliances (or covenants), it's more than just a contractual agreement. In a covenant with God, for the fullness of grace to express itself, the heart must be all in, doubled down, 200% committed. It's a match made in heaven.

When Elijah encountered God's Spirit on Mount Horeb, he regained his place in his covenant with God. Elijah was restored. He was reminded who God was in his life and who he was to God. And from that place, the prophet could rise up and move forward again with confidence. He knew who he was and what he had to do. From that place of solid reassurance – within the covenant – God told him to continue.

The Lord said to him, "Go back the way you came…"
1 Kings 19:15

After the night in the cave, after you've poured your heart out to God, he always responds and restores. Return to the struggle, he tells you. Straighten things out as best you can. Return to your life. Go anoint kings and name your successor, he told Elijah. Get back to your life's purpose. You have much more to do, and you are never alone. With the hand of God upon you, continue forward faithfully in your covenant with the Lord.

Chapter 16: The deal of a lifetime

Who wants to be happy? Sounds like a silly question, right? Doesn't everyone want to be happy? Then why is there so much unhappiness in the world? What makes people unhappy?

One way to answer this is to know what makes people happy in the first place. Medical research has actually answered this question – at least partially. Before World War II, some Harvard scientists began following a group of college students to identify what leads to healthy aging. Over time, the study grew to include people from a wide variety of backgrounds, and the research continues to this day and includes the children of the original test subjects.

After eight decades examining people's life and health, the study's central conclusion is this: good relationships keep us happier and healthier. That's it. The researchers proved that people who have close family, friends, and community relationships live longer, happier, and healthier lives. Wealth and fame have nothing to do with happiness – but loneliness kills. And for those who feel they can really count on someone when the going gets tough, their mental health stays strong as they age.

Is any of this really news? Sometimes science only proves what was already known long ago. Centuries before even Jesus walked the earth, the Lord said, *"you shall love your neighbor as yourself"* (Leviticus 19:18). In other words, good relationships are important. The Harvard scientists discovered a truth that existed from the beginning. But you already knew this too. Who needs the Bible or a university research study to tell us that our relationships matter?

There's another group of people who know this truth instinctively. Every so often in the penitentiary, we ask the prisoners to name the three most important things in life. The question generates a heated debate. But they nearly always arrive at the same conclusion. The prisoners say the most important things in life are family, health, and faith. Think about that for a second. It's amazing that for these men in jail, freedom doesn't even rank among the top three most important things.

Only once did one of them tell me money was the most important thing in life. He wasn't sure how to answer when I asked him what was more important, money or his son. Needless to say, he wasn't a very happy person. But you don't have to be in jail to have unhappy priorities. And that's where the Lord's covenant comes in.

At the most basic level, a covenant is an agreement. In a covenant, two parties agree that certain activities will or will not be carried out. Back when Moses received the tablets of the Law, a covenant was established between God and his people. The Law was a set of rules the Israelites swore to live by. Then one solemn day, Moses built an altar to commemorate the covenant between God and his people. That day, the Israelites sacrificed young bulls as offerings to the Lord, and Moses took the blood of the offerings and splashed it on the altar.

> *Then he took the book of the covenant and read it in the hearing of the people; and they said, "All that the Lord has spoken we will do, and we will be obedient." And Moses took*

the blood and threw it upon the people, and said, "Behold the blood of the covenant which the Lord has made with you in accordance with all these words."

Exodus 24:7-8

In exchange for loyalty to the Lord's covenant, God promised to bless his people and let them remain in the Promised Land. Also, keeping the covenant would set Israel apart from other nations.

"For you are a people holy to the Lord your God; the Lord your God has chosen you to be a people for his own possession, out of all the peoples that are on the face of the earth."

Deuteronomy 7:6

What happened then? Did the Israelites keep their promise and stay faithful to God? Unfortunately, not even close. Remember King Ahab, Jezebel's husband? He built an altar to Baal and promoted the worship of a pagan god. Over time, the people of Israel broke the Lord's covenant again and again. They ignored their promises, worshiped idols, and embraced corruption. The weakest in society – the widows, orphans, and immigrants – suffered greatly during this time. Some Israelites even sacrificed their children in rituals to false gods.

Inevitably, the people lost God's blessing and protection. Meanwhile, an existential threat was brewing at their border, but the Israelites didn't see it coming. They weren't prepared. Instead, they were too absorbed in themselves and their selfish ways. Coming from a nearby kingdom, the Babylonians attacked Jerusalem, and the city fell under siege. Their defenses collapsed, and the invaders destroyed the Holy Temple. After taking over Israel, the ruthless Babylonian king Nebuchadnezzar cast the people out of their homeland and sent them to live in exile. It was the darkest moment ever in the history of God's chosen people.

101

During that time, another prophet named Jeremiah appeared, and he severely criticized the Israelite leaders. He used harsh language about adultery and prostitution to describe Israel's actions in breaking its covenant with God. And Jeremiah's prophecies came true as Jerusalem was destroyed, and the people taken captive. Of course, the people were unhappy. Why? They didn't take care of their relationships – not with God and not with each other. Instead, they ignored and offended God and took advantage of the weak.

How did this happen? And why does this happen even today? Why do we turn away from God and each other even though we know that relationships are important? It all goes back to the Ten Commandments, which were written on tablets of stone. But cold, hard stone is lifeless. Even if you know the Law, that doesn't mean you'll obey it. We know it's good to be faithful, but we're not. We know telling the truth is important, but we lie. We know we should care for the weak, but we step on or ignore them instead.

In many ways, we live in a modern-day Babylon. On a macro level, it's plain to see. Our societies worship the false gods of money, fame, and power. Corruption thrives at the highest levels of government. Nations are driven by war, greed, and a lust for control – all approved under the false banner of security. They preach to us constantly about enemies and threats instead of seeking to unite and heal.

What about you and me? What about the everyday person? We too feel like we live in exile. We know something is off. We feel uneasy, and our relationships suffer. Technology isolates us with a false sense of belonging. In the past, workers felt sheltered in their office cubicles. Today, many don't even go to work, and they may never even leave their homes. With the tap of a screen, we can connect with a million people, but many of us feel lonelier than ever.

During Israel's exile, the people faced hard questions. How could God have abandoned his people? How could the Promised

Land be taken over by invaders and the Temple – God's resting place – be destroyed? Was the God of Abraham, Isaac, and Jacob truly all-powerful? But perhaps the hardest question of all was this: where did we go wrong?

How often do we behave the exact same way today? We think we can do whatever we want without consequences. We worship our selfishness and ego and then complain when we feel lonely. We think God has abandoned us, but how can we hear him if we never took the time to get to know him? The problem for the Israelites is the same problem we face today. We're all working for slavecoin*.

Slavecoin is anything that seems valuable but offers no real relationship value, and thus no true happiness – but you still work hard for it. It's all the prestige, influence, identity validation, self-image promotion, lustful pleasure, and luxury that only serve to feed our vanity and pride.

Slavecoin utilizes extensive social narratives to convince us that it holds value. But when viewed from outside its seductive force, you quickly realize slavecoin can only buy emptiness. The truth is that the people of Israel already gave themselves up to exile long before the siege of Jerusalem. The moment they turned to false gods, they entered the Babylon of the soul.

Still, even in the devastation, there is hope. And the prophet Jeremiah shows us the way.

> *Behold, the days are coming, says the Lord, when I will make a new covenant with the house of Israel and the house of Judah…*
> *…this is the covenant which I will make with the house of Israel after those days, says the Lord: I will put my law within them, and I will write it upon their hearts; and I will be their God, and they shall be my people.*

Jeremiah 31:31-33

The old covenant, which was rules-based, showed the people how often they fell short of being faithful. The Law clearly exposed their sin. In modern times, we also know the rules, and we still disobey. Our sin is also revealed. But Jeremiah tells us that God will provide a new covenant.

God says, *"I will put my law within them, and I will write it upon their hearts."* With his law written in our hearts, all we have to do then is listen to what our hearts say. And what does every heart say? Relationships matter.

A covenant is an agreement. It means each person has a responsibility to keep up their end of the bargain. But God's new covenant is radically different. Look closely. God says, *"I will"*. He doesn't put any conditions upon us even though we have sinned against him. We have sold our bodies, minds, and souls in exchange for slavecoin. But God forgives it all – and there's more.

Relationships matter to us because they matter to God. We are created in his image and likeness. And how did God decide to deepen his relationship with us? He moved closer. He came down to our level. God became human in the person of Jesus of Nazareth.

First, God showed us the rules with the Law. Next, he gave us the freedom to try it on our own. Then, after we tried and failed, he came in flesh and blood to show us how to do it. He showed us how to be more human. He showed us how to care for our relationships, and this makes us happy.

God didn't come down as an earthly king. Instead, he came down to be the last of us, the lowest. And from that place – of the weak and vulnerable, of persecuted innocence – he offers us everything. He gives us eternal life. The Messiah, King of kings and Lord of lords, did not place himself on a pedestal. Instead, he lowered himself to become sin for you and for me.

Jesus took all our idolatry, infidelity, and selfishness upon himself. God almighty was humiliated and nailed to a cross for all humankind. He took upon himself all your shame – so you don't have to be ashamed anymore. Never again. And through this tremendous outpouring of love, he writes his new covenant upon your heart.

The result? He is yours. And you are his.

This is God's new and everlasting covenant. It's a relationship that makes you unbelievably happy. But it's still a covenant, isn't it? Two parties must be involved. So, what's your part in the deal? All you have to do is let him. Let him write his story of love upon your heart.

This feels like a good place to say a prayer...

O merciful Lord,
I open my heart to you with complete trust.
Let me not be afraid anymore.
Remove the obstacles of my shame.
I know when and where I have gone wrong.
Please forgive me. I don't want that life anymore.
Write your New Covenant upon my heart, O Lord.
Free me from the chains of Babylon.
Free me to choose family, friends, health, and faith.
Let me enter into your spacious grace.
I will live in the everlasting joy of my Lord Jesus.
May he reign forever and ever in my happy heart.
Amen.

*The concept of slavecoin is adapted from: Tivy, Wolf. "Don't Learn Value From Society." Palladium Governance Futurism, July 13, 2023, https://www.palladiummag.com/2023/07/13/dont-learn-your-values-from-society/

Chapter 17: One fine spring day

For years I got rich in slavecoin. I must have been a slavecoin millionaire. Still, it didn't have to be that way. For whatever reason, I was very insecure growing up.

Maybe it was since I was smaller than other kids my age. Maybe it was my Korean heritage and physical features. I got banged around and teased a lot growing up. Maybe it's because my dad was distant, even though he loved me dearly.

The wounds I received as a child made me anxious and angry later as a young man. You would never have noticed it though. I wasn't even aware of it until much later in life. So for decades, that little boy – ashamed and alone – remained silent on the inside.

In many ways my childhood was wonderful. I was a happy kid. I remember after a long day at school, going to my friend's house and devouring his mom's freshly baked chocolate chip cookies. Every day we played street hockey, football, baseball, or basketball.

I especially loved those cool summer evenings in western Pennsylvania. We chased fireflies through backyards and over grassy hills without a care in the world. I never felt I was in danger.

I lived a privileged life. I felt free, and things seemed safer then. But looking back, I was exposed to serious risks, and eventually I embraced many of them.

Insecurity manifests itself in many ways. You might become introverted, or you might adopt narcissistic attitudes. You can become a control freak. In my case, I hid behind the masks of the partier-athlete-rebel-nerd. Yes, it was a complicated mix, but anything was allowed to protect the scared little boy inside.

Far too often I built up my ego and image around lifeless things. I invested time and energy in things that could never offer me true life value. And I explored many dark alleys. I see young people today, and I know it's even harder for many of them. They are constantly bombarded by messages of emptiness, conflict, and lost hope.

When I grew into adulthood, it got worse. Embracing risk is one thing when you're young. It's altogether different when you have adult levels of power. The web you weave can be toxic and potentially deadly.

Back then, I was a football fanatic. I remember one night; I went to a Monday Night Football game at Heinz Field. A variety of substances coursed through my veins. As I screamed and shouted at the spectacle, I remember saying out loud, "This is my church." It was a full-throated worship at the altar of Baal.

After the game, I raced home at high speeds. The passengers in my vehicle were other men close to me. I don't remember exactly how we got home – it was all a blur. Several families could have been left fatherless that night, including mine.

Back then, I was a doctor, family man, and recognized member of my community. But so much of my energy was focused on things that added no value to my relationships. I adopted lifestyles to define myself rather than having an authentic identity. I lived in a modern-day Babylonian exile of the soul.

But how could I resist the seductive message that told me we can have it all without consequences? How could the scared little boy say no to the lie that he could be strong and respected if he only worshipped Baal?

Jesus warned us about the dangers of slavecoin long ago.

> *Do not lay up for yourselves treasures on earth, where moth and rust consume and where thieves break in and steal, but lay up for yourselves treasures in heaven, where neither moth nor rust consumes and where thieves do not break in and steal. For where your treasure is, there will your heart be also.*
>
> Matthew 6:19

You might be thinking, "You were involved in wretched activity, and that's why you felt empty." And it's true. I tried to fill the vast emptiness inside with dead things. But what about the "good people"? What about those who aren't lost in superficiality?

I've met many men who I consider to be good men. They're honest, faithful, and hard working. Vices and infidelity don't contaminate their lives. They are family men. But after they've encountered Jesus along the way, something amazing happens. They leave their own personal Babylon and return to Jerusalem. They leave their own exile of their soul.

I've heard many testimonies from these men. And they all tell me the same story. You don't have to be a "bad person" to need God. These men say things like, "I never knew how empty I was inside until I found my faith. I was so tense and tired before. Now I feel light and free. And my family notices the difference. I'm so much happier now."

These guys had it all – a loving wife, kids, and steady jobs. But still, something was missing. What could it have been? Humans need relationships to thrive, right? But there are *three* relationships that matter. Jesus showed us this in his greatest commandments.

> *And one of them, a lawyer, asked him a question, to test him. "Teacher, which is the great commandment in the law?"*

And he said to him, "You shall love the Lord your God with all your heart, and with all your soul, and with all your mind. This is the great and first commandment. And a second is like it, You shall love your neighbor as yourself. On these two commandments depend all the law and the prophets."

Matthew 22:35-40

The three most important loves of your life are God, your neighbor, and yourself. If you have a solid relationship with all three, you're set. But if one of these three relationships suffer, all of them suffer.

What about the "good guys" I mentioned? Maybe, since they didn't give much attention to God, they couldn't fully give their hearts to their families. This in turn made them feel bad about themselves, hence the tension and emptiness. Others may spend a lot of time at church, but they ignore their individual or their family's needs.

Then there's the activist or crusader. They pour themselves into a worthy cause. It could be defending unborn children, working to help the poor, or caring for disabled persons. These are all noble causes that deserve our support. But what's going on in the crusader's home and in their personal relationships? What's going on in their heart? Is it all just for personal glory? Have they become so one dimensional that they've lost touch with their humanity?

If we don't love God, our neighbor, and ourselves, the final result is tragic. If you lack love for any one of the three, you may rely on a spirit of competition or control to sustain you. You can end up dehumanizing yourself and others. And when that happens, all kinds of atrocities are possible – even against yourself. Sooner or later though, everyone is given a chance to escape their exile.

I remember as a boy, praying the "Our Father" prayer over and over again during storms since the thunder and lightning terrified me. As a child, I remember believing in God. But when I entered adolescence, I stopped praying. I didn't maintain my relationship with him.

As I developed into a man on the outside, the child inside was forbidden to talk to his Father in heaven. And that made the little boy feel very lonely sometimes. He lived in exile. Meanwhile, my outer man latched on to toxic habits and attitudes. Friends and family loved me, and a loving wife and children came into my life. But without faith, I could not cherish those relationships in the way they deserved.

Then, God showed up. During my mid-30s, I began trying to clean up my act. I adopted a healthier lifestyle, and I strived to be more honest in my relationships. Looking back, I realize God was calling me even before I knew what was going on. Then something incredible happened while I was riding my bike. I didn't know it at the time, but my life was about to change dramatically as I pedaled up that steep hill heading home on a brilliant spring day. Suddenly, out of nowhere, I "heard" the Voice.

And the Lord said to me, *"You are not alone"*. These were powerful relationship words. My soul was dying to hear these words for so many years. From that moment forward, nothing would ever be the same again.

I remember my first prayer as a grown man. That night I prayed face down, the floor soaked with tears. I begged for forgiveness. Then ever so gently, God poured his mercy over me. He lifted a great weight of guilt and shame off my shoulders.

Gradually over time, the Lord helped me leave the slavecoin trade. Sometimes I'm still tempted. Sometimes I still fall. But the days of deep captivity in Babylon are long gone, thanks be to God.

One of the biggest problems we might have with relationships is that we're half-hearted about them. Yes, we can love someone, but there still might be a hard place in our hearts.

So we suffer from an uneasy feeling of distance. It's the uncomfortable, ongoing silence. It's wanting to be more open with someone, but you just can't. It's missing someone who's in the same room with you, but you don't know how to close the gap. It's feeling critical all the time... or feeling constantly judged. Or it's a strange resentment you carry inside, not knowing why. And your inner child stays curled up in a ball wanting safety and warmth, but instead the child feels cold and alone.

Meanwhile, the devil tricks us into thinking that living in harmony with God means clipping our wings. The enemy does a great job at convincing us that worldly freedom is true freedom, but all we get is slavecoin in return. And this false freedom leads us even further away from the ones we love. The accuser will give you all the external, superficial freedom in the world, as long as the inner child remains in bondage.

If we want to be truly, unconditionally free, we must embrace the entire truth. And the truth? Well, it can be kind of scary. We get a clearer picture if we identify the type of currency Jesus offers us. What are the treasures in heaven he spoke about? Here's one of my favorite explanations. It begins with the Pharisees trying to trap Jesus by asking him a question about taxes. We find this encounter in the book of Matthew.

Back then, the Romans made the Jews pay very high taxes, which bothered the people immensely. In an attempt to trap Jesus, the Pharisees asked him if he thought it was right to pay the taxes. If Jesus answered that they should not pay the tax, then the Pharisees could report this to the Roman authorities as a sign of insurrection. If Jesus said it was okay to pay the tax, they could accuse him of being disloyal to God and his people.

> *But Jesus, aware of their malice, said, "Why put me to the test, you hypocrites? Show me the money for the tax." And they brought him a coin. And Jesus said to them, "Whose likeness and inscription is this?" They said, "Caesar's." Then he said to them, "Render therefore to Caesar the things that are Caesar's, and to God the things that are God's." When they heard it, they marveled; and they left him and went away.*
> Matthew 22:18-22

You see, Jesus' economy works beyond our worldly ways. He's fully aware that our systems are frequently corrupt. He knows we're trapped in Babylon where the game is rigged by those that rule. So he says, yes, live with it the best you can. But here's the "scary" part. The coin carried the image of the Roman emperor's face, so logically it belongs to Caesar. And what image do you and I carry upon us?

> *So God created man in his own image, in the image of God he created him; male and female he created them.*
> Genesis 1:27

We carry the image of God. And this can be scary in a way. Maybe scary isn't the best word for it. Instead, it's overwhelming, tremendous, incredible, earth-shaking news. Why? Because it means we are godlike. And God wants all of us. He wants us to love him *"with all your heart, and with all your soul, and with all your mind."*

He wants you to love him with everything since that is how he loves you. Its Spirit speaking to spirit. It's love responding to Love. Nothing is held back. When you fall in love, it catches you by surprise. You might say to yourself, "I'm in love. I'm really in love! Incredible!" And it can be scary, but in a wonderful way.

That's the alliance God wants to have with you. It's an everlasting bond. It's sharing in the love between the Father, the Son, and the Holy Spirit. It's God caring for us so much that he became one of us to love us with a human heart. He came to teach us, live with us, and die for us. And in this alliance with God, you accumulate *kingdom-coin* which never rusts and can't be stolen. It's the treasure of your heart.

And when you step into God's kingdom alliance, your wings aren't clipped, not at all. Instead, it's the complete opposite. Your inner child – ashamed, afraid, and alone – is finally allowed to live again. Your soul soars free, and your relationships thrive.

But a true alliance isn't just a warm, fuzzy feeling. It's something much deeper and more solid. A relationship with Jesus is not an appendage. It's not something layered onto your life like an outfit you change. As you respond to his life-giving love, you consciously seek to saturate your life with God's presence. It's not a lifestyle but life itself. And in the next chapter, we'll look at the life of someone who lived it better than anyone.

Chapter 18: The strong heart must love

She lived in a small, nondescript town nestled among the hills of Galilee near Mount Tabor. At home that day, she waited quietly. Or perhaps she was busy doing chores in her home made of adobe, straw, and stone.

Maybe she was busy mixing leaven with a few measures of flour for the daily bread. Or maybe she was mending a garment making sure not to use a new cloth patch since it would shrink and ruin the fabric – just like her mother taught her.

What went through her mind that day? Did she sense something, anything at all? She must have. Even at her young age, she was likely a woman of great intuition. "Today is going to be a special day", she must have sensed. If so, she had no idea how special it would turn out to be.

When the angel Gabriel announced her son's birth to her, the young virgin was the first person in history to hear the name of the Son of God.

And behold, you will conceive in your womb and bear a son, and you shall call his name Jesus.   Luke 1:31

The angel brought the good news that the Messiah was coming. Her people had been waiting generations for this moment – and it was finally here! The angel's proclamation was crystal clear.

He will be great, and will be called the Son of the Most High;
and the Lord God will give to him the throne of his father David,
and he will reign over the house of Jacob forever;
and of his kingdom there will be no end.

Luke 1:32-33

This woman wouldn't just know Jesus personally. For nine months she would carry him in her womb. She would give birth to him. The young mother would nurse her child and see him take his first steps. She would wipe his tears away when he skinned his knee.

Her entire existence would revolve around her son, and she would accompany him his entire life. As a disciple, she would listen attentively to Jesus' teachings and transmit them to others. She would stay by his side until the day of his death. If anybody was ever in tune with God, it was Mary of Nazareth.

Even though she was a virgin, she was told she would conceive a son. And even though it wasn't easy to accept the news, the young woman knew it was true. The angel spoke – and Mary trusted. She believed.

"For with God nothing will be impossible."
And Mary said, "Behold, I am the handmaid of the
Lord; let it be to me according to your word."

Luke 1:37-38

Mary declared herself the "handmaid" of the Lord. Other biblical translations say "servant" or even "slave". It's an attitude of complete, undivided attention. But she was also Jesus' mother. A closer bond could never have been imagined.

115

So she journeyed to Bethlehem with her husband Joseph. And her son, the King of kings, Lord of lords was born in a stable. Shepherds appeared telling her that they had seen the glory of God and angels praising the coming of Christ. Wise men from the East came to offer her child gold, frankincense, and myrrh. It would be fair to say that Mary must have felt overwhelmed by it all.

But Mary kept all these things, pondering them in her heart.

Luke 2:19

The heart of Mary – what a wondrous, mysterious place! Later, when she presented her baby at the temple, as was the Jewish tradition, there was a man there named Simeon. He had been waiting for years for Israel to be delivered from bondage. When he looked upon Jesus, Simeon proclaimed, *"For my eyes have seen your salvation"* (Luke 2:30). But he also said something else to Mary, something that predicted future difficulty for the young mother.

"This child is destined to cause the falling and rising of many in Israel, and to be a sign that will be spoken against, so that the thoughts of many hearts will be revealed. And a sword will pierce your own soul too."

Luke 2:34-35

What might have gone through Mary's mind upon hearing these words? Did she worry? Did she doubt? Years later, when the young Jesus got lost during the Passover celebration, his parents found him in the temple, listening to the teachers and asking them questions. His understanding and intelligence amazed everyone, but his parents were worried sick. When Mary asked the boy why he didn't stay with the rest of the family, his answer puzzled the parents.

116

"Why were you searching for me?" he asked. "Didn't you know I had to be in my Father's house?" But they did not understand what he was saying to them.

Then he went down to Nazareth with them and was obedient to them. But his mother treasured all these things in her heart. And Jesus grew in wisdom and stature, and in favor with God and man.

Luke 2:49-52

She treasured all these things in her heart, it says. Later, her son would teach, *"For where your treasure is, there your heart will be also"* (Matthew 6:21).

It's natural for a mother to treasure her children, but Mary's example gives us key details about how to stay in sync with God. This is revealed in a special event that happened in the first chapter of the Gospel of Luke. While still pregnant with Jesus, Mary went to visit her relative Elizabeth who was pregnant with John who years later, as a prophet, would end up baptizing many people, including Jesus.

The baby John in Elizabeth's womb jumped for joy at hearing Mary's voice. And at that meeting – between the two expectant mothers, John the Baptist, and Jesus – one of the most important songs of praise ever burst forth from Mary's lips. Here we discover another dimension of Mary, perhaps lying dormant for many years. Here, the virgin mother reveals her familiarity with God's Word. And she sings a song of praise in a prophetic voice.

Take your time. Read Mary's song and treasure the words in your heart. Read it as if you were the one saying the words out loud.

"My soul glorifies the Lord
  and my spirit rejoices in God my Savior,
for he has been mindful
  of the humble state of his servant.
From now on all generations will call me blessed,
  for the Mighty One has done great things for me—

holy is his name.
His mercy extends to those who fear him,
   from generation to generation.
He has performed mighty deeds with his arm;
   he has scattered those who are proud in their inmost thoughts.
He has brought down rulers from their thrones
   but has lifted up the humble.
He has filled the hungry with good things
   but has sent the rich away empty.
He has helped his servant Israel,
   remembering to be merciful
to Abraham and his descendants forever,
   just as he promised our ancestors."

Luke 1:46-55

These verses must have also been familiar to her son Jesus.
They evoked the prophets and psalmists of ages ago. And they
echo the words that he would teach to the multitudes years later
during his Sermon on the Mount. Again, take your time. Read
Jesus' words with all your heart.

"Blessed are the poor in spirit, for theirs is the kingdom of heaven.
"Blessed are those who mourn, for they shall be comforted.
"Blessed are the meek, for they shall inherit the earth.
*"Blessed are those who hunger and thirst for righteousness, for
they shall be satisfied.*
"Blessed are the merciful, for they shall obtain mercy.
"Blessed are the pure in heart, for they shall see God.
"Blessed are the peacemakers, for they shall be called sons of God.
*"Blessed are those who are persecuted for righteousness' sake, for
theirs is the kingdom of heaven.*
*"Blessed are you when men revile you and persecute you and utter
all kinds of evil against you falsely on my account.*
*Rejoice and be glad, for your reward is great in heaven, for so men
persecuted the prophets who were before you."*

Matthew 5:3-12

These two passages contain tremendous secrets about how to live in spiritual harmony with God. As I mentioned earlier, being "poor in spirit" can mean that you need God so much – and you can never get enough of his love. These life-giving words are the ones God wishes to write upon our hearts.

What are the things you have saved in your heart? Maybe it's the memory of hard times you suffered. Or maybe it's something good and wholesome from your childhood. Or perhaps you remember when you failed miserably and also when you found strength you never knew you had. Mary also recalled important events in her history, which was also the history of her son.

These archives of the soul are nothing less than the richness of the life you've lived. And if we let the Holy Spirit interpret these moments, we can gain wisdom in place of bitterness. We can grow patient instead of being frustrated all the time. We can have a shot at being humble and kind. And then you realize that God has been with you all along your journey, even during the most painful moments.

If you let God in – like Mary did when she said 'yes' to the angel – then the Lord makes your heart his home. We often harden our hearts because we've been hurt, and we don't want to get hurt again. But a heart of stone can't feel anything – and if a heart can't feel, it can't love. Meanwhile, a heart of flesh, a strong muscular heart, CAN feel and it MUST love. That's what it was made to do.

Without a doubt, Mary's heart must have been incredibly strong. Consider how she must have felt when Jesus said things like:

> *"The Son of man will be delivered to the chief priests and the scribes, and they will condemn him to death, and deliver him to the Gentiles; and they will mock him, and spit upon him, and scourge him, and kill him; and after three days he will rise."*

Mark 10:33-34

When she heard this kind of talk, did Mary pull her son aside and try to convince him to tone things down? Did she tell Jesus that he should try to find an easier way to fulfill his mission? No, but Jesus' disciple Peter did, and Jesus' reaction was definitive. He didn't want to see Jesus suffer, so Peter said:

> *"God forbid, Lord! This shall never happen to you."*
> *But Jesus turned and said to Peter,*
> *"Get behind me, Satan! You are a hindrance to me; for you*
> *are not on the side of God, but of men."*
>
> Matthew 16:22-23

We all need help to stay steady during tough times. You might understand why you must go through a trial, but what if it happens to someone you love? Maybe it takes all your strength not to interfere, even though you know something tragic might occur. But you know that you can't control everything, and all you can do is trust.

It may hurt you worse than anything, waiting for a loved one who faces trouble or difficulty. Yet still, like Mary, you don't harden your heart. It's as if you yourself feel the pain of the whip and the nails driving into the flesh. Emotional pain can be just as bad, or worse, than physical pain. Still, you keep loving with the strongest of hearts despite the hurt. You can do this since your heart is open to God. And the open heart stays human, willing to feel and give of itself, despite the pain.

Mary was not exempt from this kind of suffering. She witnessed first-hand when they led her son away to be executed. When Mary looked up to her son – beaten and bloodied on the cross – perhaps she remembered those early days when she was younger: the angel announcing the coming of her Savior; the nine months carrying God's child inside her; seeing her son grow into a man, full of wisdom and grace; witnessing miracles and wonders as the power of God flowed from her son's hands to heal the sick and free the spiritually distressed.

She may have been brought to tears seeing how tender and loving her son was to those who were rejected by society. Until finally, they tied him up and dragged him away to prison... and sentenced him to death. What could the mother of Jesus have felt at that moment? What did her heart, wide open to God, feel at the crucifixion? Simeon's prophecy said it all.

"And a sword will pierce your own soul." And as it pierced her soul, it pierced her heart, where her treasure, Jesus Christ, remained.

Chapter 19: More than the universe

In the last chapter, we looked at how the servant of the Lord, Mother Mary, remained in tune with God. Now let's see how her son, Jesus did things.

It's well known how he embraced the poor, sick, and marginalized. He always put those who were excluded and shunned at the center of his attention. He ministered to the sick and the sinners. And Jesus had no problem touching and healing lepers, despite it being prohibited by the law. With his actions, Jesus showed us clearly where God's priorities are.

But beyond the miracles and healings, to truly understand Jesus, I believe we must look at his actions in more intimate settings. In gatherings with his inner circle, what did Jesus do and say? In moments of solitude, what did his attitude look like? And what about when he struggled with deep personal issues? During these moments, we can certainly learn a lot from the only man who was in tune with God at all times.

One of the most intimate things people can do is share a meal. So, we're invited to the Last Supper. Jesus' final meal with his apostles wasn't just any occasion. It was the last time that he would meet with his 12 closest disciples prior to his death. It was a hugely important moment for Jesus and his followers.

On that occasion, a great source of spiritual nourishment was about to be given by the Son of God. That night, a practice would be established that would last for centuries until this day. And it all started with a simple gesture.

> *Jesus, knowing that the Father had given all things into his hands, and that he had come from God and was going to God, rose from supper, laid aside his garments, and girded himself with a towel. Then he poured water into a basin, and began to wash the disciples' feet, and to wipe them with the towel with which he was girded.*
>
> John 13:3-5

Trying to fully understand God is impossible. Our galaxy, the Milky Way, contains up to 400 billion stars. And there may be up to two trillion galaxies in the observable universe. You and I are tiny dots of flesh clinging to a speck of dirt floating in the cosmos. Who could possibly even begin to understand the Creator of the universe? We have enough trouble understanding ourselves sometimes. Still, God had a plan for us since the beginning.

Since we need him so much, and since he wants us to know his love, God came down to earth. He came down to our level, face to face. And from there, he kneeled at our feet – even at the feet of those who would betray him.

The Messiah knew that within a short time, Judas would leave to tell the authorities where Jesus was to arrest him. But instead of waiting until Judas left, Jesus washed his betrayer's feet and the feet of the other apostles. Many months before, after a long night of prayer, Jesus chose the Twelve, and Judas was one of them. Did he name Judas as part of his innermost circle by mistake? Can the Son of God make a mistake?

I believe one reason Jesus chose Judas was to reveal to us something incredible – that is, the depths of God's love. And it's even bigger than the universe. We are always free to reject it or embrace it, but God's love never leaves.

God's love has no pride or pretense. It only desires to serve the good of the other. And the real-world manifestation of this love must be humble. This was a central message of Jesus' teaching all along, and it came to life at that very moment.

If we look closer, several layers of depth open up to us. The scriptures say that Jesus *"laid aside his garments"*, that is, he stripped down to wash the apostles' feet. Why would he do this? Those who lived during those times would understand intuitively why Jesus did this.

By exposing himself, Jesus took on the appearance of a servant, or slave. In biblical times, the washing of feet was customary as people wore sandals and accumulated dirt on their feet. As house guests, each individual would wash their own feet, or a servant would do it for them.

Take a step back and think about this scene. What does it say to you? The wisest, most holy individual, God-as-man, on his knees, washing the feet of everyday people, sinners, and even traitors. The Creator of our multi-trillion-star universe reduced himself to the role of a slave. This turns our entire world vision upon its head.

In Jesus' time and today, so much messaging emphasizes prestige, influence, and power. And with digital media, society has grown more superficial than ever. So much revolves around personal image and appearances. Even when striving to do good, some may only seek recognition and applause. But on the night of the Last Supper, we find the God-man, the Almighty and All-Powerful on his knees, half-naked, doing a slave's work.

How does this challenge you? It challenges me to the core. Jesus says to me, *"Forget about everything you know about how to get things done. Because before you can even do the simplest task, like washing someone's feet, you must have the right attitude, the correct spirit. Any notion of superiority spoils it."* For some, including me, it's hard to break free of feeling above others sometimes, especially when we're in positions of power. What's even more challenging is what Jesus later asks of his disciples, and of us.

> *When he had washed their feet, and taken his garments, and resumed his place, he said to them, "Do you know what I have done to you? You call me Teacher and Lord; and you are right, for so I am. If I then, your Lord and Teacher, have washed your feet, you also ought to wash one another's feet.*
>
> John 13:12-14

At that moment, the disciples might have been thinking, "That's a lot to ask. I don't know if I can do what the Master wants of me. Does he really want me to humiliate myself down to the level of a slave?" It's not about letting people boss you around. And it's not about being subservient to other people's whims no matter what they ask.

Instead, Jesus wants us to abandon our selfish nature. He knows how hard it is for us to do this. That's why he used such a graphic example. Wash their feet, he tells us. This is what true service looks like. This is the attitude required. It should include visible acts of kindness. Strive to make it as real as possible. The goal isn't to call attention, but rather to open yourself up to God's galaxy-generating love to transform you into a truly humble servant.

With his example, the Lord shows us how to break down the power structures that dehumanize our world today. This is how God wants us to respond to the attitudes and actions that harm our families and communities. He wants faithful servants that will set aside their ego and let the Spirit of God do his good work through us and in us.

It means rolling up your sleeves and getting into the weeds and the mud sometimes. It's getting down on your hands and knees to cleanse a wound or scrub a toilet if needed. Even if you're in charge of a family, team, or company you can still have the servant attitude. It means seeking the best for all those involved.

Then you're not focused on advancing your career at all costs or extracting excess work out of people. Instead, you get down to their level, or even below them in a spirit of service. You seek to understand their struggles and their joys. You leave selfishness behind.

Maybe you weren't so humble when you started your journey, but a change can appear along the way. You can develop a desire to serve. And as you remain in that position of service, humility has a chance to take shape in you. God's Spirit can work in you and through you – just like Jesus. Being in sync with him is being like him. And the result? Again, Jesus was very specific.

> *For I have given you an example, that you also should do as I have done to you. Truly, truly, I say to you, a servant is not greater than his master; nor is he who is sent greater than he who sent him. If you know these things, blessed are you if you do them.*
>
> John 13:15-17

Chapter 20: Does God want human sacrifice?

After the washing of the feet, the main event of Jesus' last meal with his disciples was about to take place. Again, this was a moment of profound intimacy with his followers. Within hours, Jesus would be handed over to the authorities to begin the final phase of his life before his death.

Jesus shared many meals with his apostles over the years, but this time it was different. There's no doubt they sensed something exceptional was taking place. After the washing of the feet, the weight of the moment was undeniable. There was no joking or small-talk going on. A feeling of anticipation hung in the air.

Jesus did not want his apostles to forget any details about that night. And the disciples fed on every word that fell from the lips of their Master. That evening, Jesus instituted the Eucharist, also known as the Lord's Supper.

> *Now as they were eating, Jesus took bread, and blessed, and broke it, and gave it to the disciples and said, "Take, eat; this is my body." And he took a cup, and when he had given thanks he gave it to them, saying, "Drink of it, all of you; for*

this is my blood of the covenant, which is poured out for many
for the forgiveness of sins.

Matthew 26:26-28

In the Book of Lucas, Jesus also names the *"new covenant"* at the Last Supper. And he reminds the apostles to *"Do this in remembrance of me."*

During the final meal with his apostles, Jesus revealed to them, and to us, key elements to remain united in the Spirit with him. Here, God's covenant begins to evolve into its fullest expression as the apostles come into deeper communion with his Son.

Carefully consider the words Jesus used. Read them slowly. Meditate upon them. Feed upon the words like the disciples did.

He gave thanks.

Take, eat; this is my body.

Drink of it, all of you;

This is my blood of the covenant which is poured out for the forgiveness of sins.

Do this in memory of me.

You don't share meals with just anyone. You don't sit down to break bread, especially in private settings, unless the other person is close to you. Meals eaten with loved ones are of supreme importance to us. A shared meal reveals a lasting bond.

And at the Last Supper, in a few short phrases, Jesus revealed the spiritual code for living in tune with God. Incorporating these truths would be essential for the disciples back then and for Christians of every age.

To this day, we continue to embrace these truths to be in communion with our Creator. In memory of Christ, we gather at his table to celebrate. And it all points towards Jesus' resurrection. In his words and actions, in the breaking of the bread and the sharing of the cup, Jesus reveals to us the key elements to eternal life.

The Lord made it very clear what the New Covenant with him was all about. *"This is my blood of the covenant, which is poured out for many for the forgiveness of sins"*, he said. He explicitly links the spilling of his blood to forgiveness. When we are forgiven by him, in the spilling of his blood, we enter into communion with him. But this might cause confusion for some.

Some people criticize the Christian faith because of the belief that Jesus died for our sins. They say things like, "If God is merciful and kind, why would he send his Son to his death? Why should Jesus have to die for my mistakes? Does God want human sacrifice?"

The problem with these questions is that they want to place the Creator of the universe in a box. They try to give God human-like motives, methods, and limitations. If taken at face value, yes, the idea of God's innocent son dying for our sins might cause some intellectual dilemmas. But God's plans are much more magnificent than we could ever imagine. And we are infinitely limited in his presence. We can recall the words of the prophet Isaiah:

> *For my thoughts are not your thoughts,*
> *neither are your ways my ways, says the Lord.*
> *For as the heavens are higher than the earth,*
> *so are my ways higher than your ways*
> *and my thoughts than your thoughts.*
>
> Isaiah 55:8-9

There are many theological and philosophical explanations for why Jesus' death was necessary. We broke away from God time after time. Every time we turn our back on someone; every time we are selfish, cruel, and unkind; every time we lie, cheat, or steal

– we do it to him. And to return to him, it requires something monumental – an unmistakable outpouring of mercy.

The reasons reach back to the Garden of Eden, Exodus, the Torah (the Law), and the animal sacrifices at the Temple in Jerusalem. These explanations provide the Christian faith with solid fundamentals which have built up church teaching for centuries. And the Holy Spirit speaks forcefully through these teachings.

These fundamentals are eternally relevant, and centuries of God's Word back it up when you want to explore more. But even the most basic knowledge of the New Covenant can and must be life changing.

If I can't receive it with my heart, then understanding it with my head won't be enough. If I can't quickly grasp the essence of Jesus' mission at a gut level, then all the theology in the world won't help me. It must work within the context of my life here and now.

And what is the essence of his message? I have sinned against God, others, and myself. Jesus spilled his blood for me. He died for me. And for this, my sins are forgiven. He rose from the dead as proof. For some, that might not be enough of an explanation. But for me, it's everything.

Today's world is so complicated. It's hard to find the truth about anything anymore. So many corrupt powers and selfish interests distort our modern narratives. There's too much information out there to process in a single lifetime. But if there is one truth that can give me lasting hope, what could it be?

God sent his Son. He died for me out of love for me and for you. And if that truth pierces our heart and takes root in our soul, it must be transforming.

This is the greatest truth of all time. It's an indestructible diamond that you carry with you. It leads to faith like steel. It's food and drink for your weary soul. And if you are nourished by the Lord's flesh and blood, then your communion with him will thrive.

This is the blood covenant that Jesus spoke about and established at the Last Supper. To be in tune with him we should participate. His words were clear.

Eat. Drink. Be forgiven. Remember.

Later, Jesus' actions would crystalize these words forever in the hearts and minds of his followers for centuries until the modern age.

Chapter 21: The sleepless night

In many ways my writing here has been an experiment, like I said, a kind of spiritual laboratory. Even though this book is about living in syntony with God, this doesn't mean it's something I've mastered. Still, I try. I've had glimpses of it, and I know I want more. And for you, dear reader, I'm sure you are trying too. We all do our best. But what happens when we face hard situations that we didn't ask for, or don't deserve?

Over the centuries, philosophers and spiritual thinkers have tried to figure out why evil and suffering exist. We know that in the Garden of Eden, Adam and Eve rebelled against God. Some say that bad things happen because human sin contaminated the earth. This set off a chain reaction that continues to cause all types of maladies today. We've also heard that since he loves us, God gives us freedom to choose between good and evil. And many times, we choose to hurt ourselves or others. You might have also heard that evil is the absence of love.

Others say that evil and suffering exist to give us a chance to make a difference. So we can try to right the wrongs and relieve the pain. Other lines of thought say, if the world was perfect, without suffering, everything would be lifeless. Without suffering, everyone would be the same. So in many ways, our pain defines us.

While these explanations make some sense, do any of them help me during those sleepless nights when I'm worried or afraid? Philosophical perspectives might interest me, but when my heart and soul are breaking, what answer does God give me? When Job asked about these things, God's answer was authoritative. Get over it. I'm God. You can't understand the Creator of all that exists.

The Book of Job is one of the oldest books in the Bible. Some even say it was written before Genesis. It's no surprise that these two ancient texts deal with the concepts of suffering and sin. We can groan all we want, but the galaxies will keep spinning. Suns will be born and go dark in an instant. We can't change any of this.

Even though Job finally accepted this reality – and even though it's an absolute truth – I'm not sure a "deal-with-it-I'm-the-boss" explanation works for me. I need more during my sleepless nights. God knows this too. And his response is remarkable.

Before he began his public ministry, Jesus ventured into the desert. The Gospel says Jesus was driven into the desert by the Spirit (Mark 1:12). According to many ancient traditions, the desert is a place of purification and preparation. It's a place where you must leave your comfort zone. In the desert, the Son of God confronted Satan and his temptations. Jesus had to go through this trial before he began his mission. He had to face down the demon first.

The devil tempted Jesus to turn stones into bread to soothe his hunger. But Jesus chose to depend on God's Word to nourish him instead.

Jesus was also tempted to throw himself off the roof of the temple to prove that God kept him safe. But Jesus chose not to foolishly test God's protection.

Satan also tempted Jesus to take control over all the nations. But instead, he chose to live among the people as one of them and to serve them from a position of humility (Matthew 4:1-11).

In resisting temptation, Jesus showed us the way of a loyal servant-master that only worships God. But even those 40 days and nights in the desert were nothing compared to what Jesus eventually faced that sleepless night after the Last Supper.

That evening, he took three of his disciples to pray with him in the garden of Gethsemane. Even God's Son needed some company that night. Jesus knew he was about to face the hardest trial of his life.

> *Then he said to them, "My soul is very sorrowful, even to death; remain here, and watch with me."*
>
> Matthew 26:38

Here we have the man who could never be out of sync with God, experiencing sorrow so intense that it felt like death. Some Christians like to use the suffering of Jesus to make us feel bad. They may even say things like, "See! Look what you did to poor Jesus. It's all your fault. Confess and repent now!"

Perhaps this does have some meaning for us. We *have* sinned. We *should* repent when we've done wrong. From Eden to Exodus to modern day times, we've done things we never should have done. And many times, the innocent pay the price. But the real message goes far beyond this. The work of Jesus was not meant to establish a relationship of guilt with God.

How many times have you had to deal with contradictions in your life? How often have you had to face problems that you didn't create? How many times have you had to deal with the mistakes of others? Have you ever looked into your own heart and disliked what you found there? Who hasn't? I certainly have.

This brings the question of suffering into sharper focus. Yes, some of it is our own fault. We've made mistakes, we've been cruel and unkind. We have sinned against God and our neighbor. But it's not all our fault as individuals. Sometimes suffering arrives completely uninvited at your doorstep. And sometimes entire communities or nations can journey down the wrong path.

Still, while we may agree with the concept of collective fault or the mistakes of society, it doesn't make us feel any better when a loved one gets sick. Ideas don't help you when someone you care about makes bad choices or when you must deal with toxic people. Some can even make life miserable for you – and it's not your fault at all. These circumstances can cause us deep pain, especially when they involve someone close to us.

The night after the Last Supper, a dear friend of Jesus would betray him. At a critical moment, Peter, the leader of the apostles, would publicly deny knowing Jesus. His followers would scatter and abandon him. That night, Jesus would be arrested, falsely accused, imprisoned, tortured, and executed the next day. The perverse marriage between corrupt religious and political power would kill him. And he saw it coming. Jesus made prophecies about his death all throughout his ministry.

Things don't always turn out the way you want. Some trials are terribly painful. And explanations about Adam and Eve or the Creator of the universe won't calm your heart. But what if it's true that God's Son came to earth for you? What if somehow you knew, deep down, that no matter what, Jesus is at your side? He shares your hurt. He knows all about contradiction, frustration, and even fear. And he is there for you in the most human and humble way possible. That night Jesus said:

> *"Father, if thou art willing, remove this cup from me; nevertheless not my will, but thine, be done."*
> Luke 22:42

At that moment, in his own way, Jesus questioned his Father. He openly expressed doubt about dying for all our sins. He thought about avoiding the shame, humiliation, and excruciating pain. And God's answer? Silence. How many times have you received the same answer in your questions and your prayers? But this doesn't mean God is absent. Instead, he is there, fully present at your side. *Jesus was his own answer.* He knew and accepted that it had to be this way.

And as we continue along this spiritual experiment, I feel the entire world cries out for answers now. War after war breaks out. Nations are fiercely divided. The horrors of evil and suffering have never been displayed in such an explicit way on a global scale. We can watch the graphic expression of our depravity 24/7 on a tiny little screen in the palm of our hand. And given our capacity for destruction, our abuse of free will could reach apocalyptic proportions. It's as if the entire world is entering into a sleepless night.

There are countless political and historical excuses for the conflicts happening now. The finger pointing is endless, but one thing is for sure. Deep rage has been unleashed on the battlefield and in the streets. Many desire the utter destruction of others in the name of vengeance. Empty promises of prosperity, security, and peace have been exposed for all the world to see. And as always, the weak and vulnerable suffer the most for our sins.

The tragic events happening today give us a notion about the evil that was unleashed upon and absorbed by Christ. But we only see a snapshot of it. The Son of Man took all the atrocities, across all time, forever, upon himself.

For Jesus, his prayer in Gethsemane was a pivotal moment in the history of salvation. He was offered the opportunity to forgive all sin forever – but he could have said 'no'. Jesus knew it would extract a heavy price. And the pressure upon him was enormous.

And being in anguish, he prayed more earnestly, and his sweat was like drops of blood falling to the ground.

Luke 22:44

So perhaps we find ourselves, with Jesus, on our knees in prayer in the garden. None of us need more war to make life harder. We all have plenty to deal with while facing our own trials. And for some, all the wars and catastrophes don't matter, not even a tiny bit, since their own personal reality is a living hell.

So can we remain faithful despite the contradictions we see all around us? Can we see past the pain and still trust God? So many have been pushed into the line of fire due to circumstances beyond their control. And for every innocent life lost, God holds us all accountable. We are all accomplices in some form of cruelty, corruption, and injustice.

But instead of unleashing his wrath, God holds back his hand. Instead, he sends his Son. He sends mercy. And it's Jesus that drinks from the bitter cup filled with the wrath of God against all the suffering and sin in the world. He did this for you and for me… for all of us. He consumes it all to the last drop. And this gives us hope against hope. If we look hard enough, past the smoke and flames, we can see redemption on the horizon.

In the face of the worst injustice of all, aimed directly against him, where did Jesus go? He sought refuge in his Father's will, no matter how hard it was to accept. Despite his anguish, the Son's faith in his Father's love was unbreakable. So Jesus not only provides us with a real-world example, but he also embodies the salvation that otherwise escapes us.

In Jesus, we find our inspiration *and* our salvation. In him there is no failure, even when we fail. If you think about one person bearing all our sins upon him, it's astonishing. But he didn't do this as some kind of invincible superhero. He did it as a vulnerable human being. He did it out of the purest love of all time. And this inspires us and humbles us into trusting him.

All this helps me to face the contradictions in my own life, because I can't fix it myself. Nobody can. But Jesus gives himself to us in our struggle. It had to be God, in human form, to show us how and to save us. And in the vast emptiness of our failure a wide-open space appears where God's grace can act.

Why do evil and suffering exist? What's God's answer? The only answer I've found – the only one that makes sense to my heart – is a Person.

Jesus Christ gives me a flesh and blood, human answer to face down sin and death. And the only way is to keep striving to live, in communion with God, come what may.

There's a wealth of spiritual insight found in Jesus' prayer in the garden. But there's another person who appears on the scene who gives us another perspective we might never have thought of. So let's follow the Lord's command and warning.

"Rise! Let us go! Here comes my betrayer!"

Matthew 26:46

Chapter 22: The meadows of grace

"He's going to ruin everything!" he screamed in his head. "This is not how it's supposed to be. How can I change all this?" And his mind raced around in circles, trying to figure out an angle, like he did so many times in the past.

Then, in a flash, it came to him. And in his tortured mind, he hatched a plan. "Yes. I'll go to them. That's it. They will take care of it for me." So he stormed off into the night. Later, he came face to face with the chief priests. And Judas Iscariot made a deal for thirty pieces of silver to hand over Jesus to the authorities.

I don't know how it feels to be 100% in sync with God. But I do know how it feels to be out of sync with him. In my own way, I know how it feels to be like Judas. What follows here might not be based on solid theological reasoning. But like I said, I know a thing or two about Jesus' betrayer.

Back in the day when I roamed far from God, my thoughts were incredibly self-centered. When I look back, I was like a rat in a cage, completely consumed by my selfish desires. It's incredibly painful to live this way. Constant turmoil boils within you, and all you think about is what you want and how to get it.

Although I received love, my goals back then were shallow. Superficial desires and materialism drove my actions. The world programmed me to think that way, and a certain level of obsession whipped me into action, even a frenzy sometimes. And the thing I lacked most of all was peace.

So I imagine Judas. I picture a man who took advantage of his place among the apostles. I envision an ambitious individual who waited in the wings, always looking for an opportunity. The Book of John says that Judas was a thief and that he stole from the ministry's money box.

Imagine hearing the Son of God preach the Sermon on the Mount. Imagine seeing him perform miracles and life transformations. Maybe you even saw him walk on water. But despite having seen and heard it all, you lie, cheat, and steal anyway. You rob from the ministry's savings. This could only happen in a heart as cold as ice – a lonely, hardened heart.

Like I said, I know a thing or two about Judas. I know what a selfish heart is capable of. Some might say the cold-hearted only care about themselves, but it's not true. Loving care has nothing to do with it. Instead, a dark spirit of control lurks behind it all.

It's the same spirit that caused Lucifer to be cast out of heaven. You want to be like God. Or even worse, you think you can do a better job than God. For me, it started with personal wounds I wanted to keep hidden. It hurt me too much to look at them. So I covered up the hurt with my vanity and pride.

Did someone hurt Judas when he was just a boy? Maybe something in his past drove him to do whatever he wanted to soothe the pain. Some say he counted on Jesus to be a powerful, military Messiah. And when things didn't go according to Judas' expectations, he handed Jesus over to the authorities.

Perhaps the apostle thought, yes, Jesus is the Messiah. But maybe Judas felt he had to force Jesus's hand by stirring up conflict. Then Judas would get what he wanted, that is, Jesus calling his heavenly army to fight. Or maybe Judas was simply a petty thief, taking advantage of the ministry out of greed. Either way, it's all about manipulation and control. It's being tied up in your mind, completely blocking out the voice of God.

Ironically, being selfish has nothing to do with what's good for you. It's the exact opposite. This type of existence damages your relationships, which makes you sad. But something grips you, and it won't let go. In the scriptures, it says that Satan entered Judas. When you close your heart to God, the evil one has his way with you.

The devil tells you, yes, you can have it all with no consequences. If you want control over all things, go for it. Don't worry, you don't have to respect any boundaries. Money, power, and pleasure will keep you happy, safe, and free from the pain that haunts you. But as a master of deceit, Satan never delivers on his promises. Instead, you end up tormented and tied up in the devil's lies which end up becoming your own. Take a look at this passage as an illustration.

> *There they made him a supper; Martha served, and Laz'arus was one of those at table with him. Mary took a pound of costly ointment of pure nard and anointed the feet of Jesus and wiped his feet with her hair; and the house was filled with the fragrance of the ointment. But Judas Iscariot, one of his disciples (he who was to betray him), said, "Why was this ointment not sold for three hundred denarii and given to the poor?" This he said, not that he cared for the poor but because he was a thief, and as he had the money box he used to take what was put into it.*
>
> John 12:2-6

We see how some people assume postures of virtue, but deep inside, they only think about themselves. How many campaigns and causes do we see perverted by this kind of attitude? From the left, right, and center – both religious and secular – they shout about virtue and justice, but deep down all they want to do is satisfy their egos. They lie to themselves and say it's good to do bad, as long as you look good and get a bit of glory.

Some may wonder, how could God let this happen? Why did Jesus pick Judas as an apostle? Was the betrayal an intentional act of God? Couldn't he have come up with a better plan? Maybe in his mind, Judas asked similar questions. He doubted God's motives and methods.

Maybe there's a simpler way to see things. Judas was filled with resentment and remorse. In an environment like that, love withers and dies. And from there, you might even sell your soul and condemn the innocent.

> *While he was still speaking, Judas, one of the Twelve, arrived. With him was a large crowd armed with swords and clubs, sent from the chief priests and the elders of the people. Now the betrayer had arranged a signal with them: "The one I kiss is the man; arrest him." Going at once to Jesus, Judas said, "Greetings, Rabbi!" and kissed him.*
> *Jesus replied, "Do what you came for, friend."*

Matthew 26:47-50

Even though Jesus knew exactly what was going on, he still called Judas his friend. And they were friends, at least Jesus thought so. He chose Judas. He spent time with him, guided him, and broke bread with him. He trusted him with missionary work and with the ministry's finances. And Jesus gently washed Judas' feet at the Last Supper.

If anyone misunderstands God's patience and mercy, these examples leave no doubt. And this makes us uncomfortable. We want Jesus to wake up and take charge. We want him to set things right and deal out justice. We want the Lord to do things the way we think they should be done. Just like Judas.

How hard it is for us to accept that we don't have it all figured out. We struggle to be at peace when things aren't the way we want

142

them to be. We reject the fact that we don't have all the answers. And in the end, we may even reject forgiveness, if it means giving up control.

Once Judas saw the results of his actions, he felt bitter remorse. But didn't he know he could be forgiven? Jesus practiced and preached this incessantly. Judas saw, with his own eyes, how the Messiah welcomed the worst of all sinners. But still, Judas' mind remained locked from the inside.

Maybe at a young age, Judas lost any notion of childlike innocence and wonder. He locked up the little boy inside him. It's foolish and immature to trust God, he might have thought. And maybe, deep down, Jesus' teaching irritated him since it meant taking a leap of faith. It meant relinquishing control.

> *"Let the children come to me, do not hinder them; for to such belongs the kingdom of God. Truly, I say to you, whoever does not receive the kingdom of God like a child shall not enter it."*

Mark 10:14-15

The faith of a child isn't held back by inhibition and fear. Instead, the childlike spirit runs free in meadows of grace. Their minds don't race, and they don't obsess over things. They don't lock themselves away seeking a false sense of security. The children of God know their Father, and he watches over them. The sons and daughters of God rest in his presence even when things get rough.

To enter into harmony with God, we must identify the things that bind us. We can ask the Spirit to help us find those structures encrusted deep within our personalities. We can ask the Lord to untangle the knots within our souls.

You might be tied up by cruelty, sarcasm, or a feeling of superiority. Or it could be playing the victim or a false sense of humility. Maybe it's apathy, laziness, or a constant demand for perfection. Nothing is ever good enough. Nothing ever satisfies. So we rage against ourselves and against God.

If you don't identify these attitudes, they can lead to major difficulty later. To detect them, pay special attention when you make a mistake. Our own errors can bring out the worst in us since we don't want to face our weakness. We double-down on our pride and refuse to seek restoration.

Judas eventually recognized he was wrong when they took Jesus into custody. The betrayer even tried to return the money he received from the chief priests. But deep down, Judas did not believe in the wide-open level of forgiveness offered by Jesus.

Finally, Judas made a choice. He decided to remain tangled up in his web of remorse even though he knew there was a way out. In the end, Judas tangled himself up literally, with a rope, and hung himself. Why didn't Judas seek forgiveness? Was it arrogance? Pride? Ego? I sometimes see in myself these tendencies that try to block out God's mercy. Then I end up hurting myself and others.

To different degrees, these attitudes can be found inside of all of us. They may even have been passed down to us through generations. Some tendencies and behaviors are inherited. In any case, we need to dig down and yank them out by the root then nail them to the cross with Christ. Only then can we truly be healed. Only then can we truly roam free in his meadows of his grace.

Chapter 23: The two Messiahs

For many, Jesus' message is absurd. Think about it. Who wants to follow him to the cross? His disciples certainly didn't. Most of them scattered and ran away.

His right-hand man, Peter – who declared Jesus as the Messiah and the Son of God – swore that he would die for the Lord. But when the chips were down, the apostle swore that he did not know him. Peter denied Jesus three times. What happened to Peter? Was he afraid? Ashamed?

Whatever the reason, he didn't want to get anywhere near the horrific reality of the cross. Who does? Why is an instrument of torture used as the universal Christian symbol of faith? Isn't that foolish?

In the eyes of the so-called wise and rational world, there's no way to accept the cross at face value. Who wants to suffer and die, much less for the faults of others? Nobody. Would you tell someone to take the blame for someone else's crime? No. That would be foolish advice, wouldn't it?

But in Jesus' "foolish" decision we encounter something extraordinary. Saint Paul expressed it this way:

For the message of the cross is foolishness to those who are perishing, but to us who are being saved it is the power of God.

1 Corinthians 1:18

How does foolishness become the power of God? When it saves you. And if embracing the cross means your salvation, then it would be foolish to reject it.

In an earlier chapter, we talked about how Moses had limitations. Jesus did too. He was fully human. Not everybody who heard his message believed in him. His preaching did not transform hearts 100% of the time. In his hometown of Nazareth, they were so skeptical of Jesus that he performed only a few miracles there (Mark 6:4-6).

Even though he preached and practiced the literal Word of God, many rejected Jesus. Some hated him, and others wanted to kill him. That night after Judas betrayed him, Jesus ended up arrested, beaten, and humiliated. Is this what being in the flow with God looks like? Sometimes in life, no matter how much faith we have, we reach a hard stop. Just like Jesus.

I feel that one of the greatest messages of the Gospel has nothing to do with changing the world – at least not the way we think it should be done. Instead, it shows us how to confront reality with our faith still intact. When we accept what appears to be foolish in the eyes of the world, then we create space for the power of God to act through us, with us, and in us.

But where does this power come from? What are its origins? To understand this, we must return to Babylon one last time. Because way back then, the Messiah had already come.

We recall that after a series of devastating sieges, the city of Jerusalem was forced to surrender. The people of Israel were taken into captivity by the Babylonian king Nebuchadnezzar II. And God's people lived in exile for nearly 50 years (some say it was 70 years).

146

An entire generation lived without a homeland, and they continuously faced the reality that Jerusalem had been destroyed. Many people were born, lived, and died in captivity. And the prophets proclaimed over and over that it was the people's fault for having worshiped false gods.

Still, there was hope, and a prophecy, that they would be delivered by the Messiah. And their hope was answered with the arrival of Cyrus the Great. Cyrus is recognized by historians as one of the most powerful and influential kings in human history.

King Cyrus wasn't even part of the nation of Israel. Cyrus was from Persia, which is now part of modern-day Iran. This king led the campaign to finally break Babylon's control and free the Jewish people from captivity.

Cyrus was well-known for having respected the customs and religious traditions of the lands that he conquered. God named Cyrus his 'anointed one', which can also mean Messiah. The prophet Isaiah tells us that the Lord unleashed great power during the reign of Cyrus. And this power eventually comes to us as well.

This is what the Lord says to his anointed,
*   to Cyrus, whose right hand I take hold of*
to subdue nations before him
*   and to strip kings of their armor,*
to open doors before him
*   so that gates will not be shut:*
I will go before you
*   and will level the mountains;*
I will break down gates of bronze
*   and cut through bars of iron.*
                                        Isaiah 45:1-2

Following his conquest of Babylon, Cyrus issued the Edict of Restoration, in which he authorized and encouraged the return of the Jewish people to the former Kingdom of Judah. This officially ended the Babylonian captivity. Hooray!

Again, Cyrus wasn't part of the tribe of Israel. He was an outsider. But he was chosen to deliver the people and show that God could use any instrument to get things done. And King Cyrus is considered to be a Christ-like figure.

Cyrus the Great founded the Achaemenid dynasty in 550 BC. It was the largest empire the world had ever seen at its time, covering a total of 5.5 million square kilometers (2.1 million square miles). King Cyrus had liberated the Jewish nation. He conquered many lands, and he showed favor towards the nation of Israel. Cyrus was the living definition of a political-military messiah.

In comparison, the one true Messiah came for something much greater than a mere political victory that would be forgotten with time. Jesus Christ came to establish an eternal kingdom with no end. But why did they follow him? Why did they follow that poor Nazarene all those centuries ago? What were they expecting? When the multitudes came to hear the words of the preacher, they didn't get stirred up. He never incited any shouting, marching, or flag waving. Instead, there was peace. There was calm. And there was power.

Later, when the crowds closed in on him and clamored after him like a rock star, Jesus called them an "evil generation" (Luke 11:29). If the people weren't interested in a change of heart, or if all they wanted was to see miracles, then they missed the Messiah's message completely.

Jesus preached all that was good about God. He gave hope to the downtrodden. He told them God was on their side, and that yes, one day there will be a judgment. But for now, the Word of God had become flesh and was standing right in front of them. The Holy Spirit was working in their hearts, minds, and souls. And all this made the authorities uneasy. Later, when his followers cheered the Nazarene upon entering Jerusalem in triumph, many hoped for a military victory. But instead, Jesus went to the cross.

If we examine the scriptures, Jesus spent nearly all his time praying, healing, and teaching. He answered criticism with authority. And he chased the money changers out of the temple since they had forgotten how to respect his Father's house. But most of Jesus' actions were spent among the people, with the poor in spirit, and they followed him in droves.

This made Jesus a threat to the system. Many others during his time also faced a similar fate, but none of them were the Messiah. Crucifixion was used to punish enemies of the state, agitators, and those with no civil rights. In the news of his day, Jesus' death was not remarkable. What made his death unique occurred on an entirely different level.

Jesus did not cry out for a temporary, superficial political change. Even the great Babylon and Cyrus' massive kingdom both faded away into history. The overthrow of one system always leads to another and then another. All governments and systems eventually become Babylon, and if we place all our faith and trust there, then we commit idolatry. No government or nation is God.

Jesus' message was simple. Believe in him. Receive God's mercy. Stop sinning. Stop the hypocrisy. Go right now and help your neighbor. Make disciples and share the Good News. Love one another.

So if Jesus wasn't calling for a military revolution, why did the authorities feel threatened? Because if enough people truly followed his words, many power structures would crumble. People would want less and therefore consume less. There would be less money to be made in killing machines and incarceration. Corruption would wither and die. Perhaps the authorities only sensed this intuitively. Either way, they perceived Jesus as a threat, and he was, but not in the way they expected.

Go back and read the Sermon on the Mount (Matthew 5-7). Where is the political manifesto? It's not there, at least not in an obvious way. Instead, Jesus demands that all political systems justify their behavior. And deep down, that's what they truly could not accept.

Jesus asks all of us to justify our individual behavior too, and he knows we fail many times. This is why he went to the cross. It goes far beyond seeking a temporary societal change. Instead, Jesus' mission is to save the world.

Perhaps the most profound irony of the Bible is the official judgment passed on Jesus that led to the death penalty. It turns out that Jesus was condemned for his claims that he was the Messiah, the Son of God, and equivalent to God. In the end, Jesus was put to death for telling the truth.

> *The high priest said to him, "I charge you under oath by the living God: Tell us if you are the Messiah, the Son of God."*
>
> *"You have said so," Jesus replied. "But I say to all of you: From now on you will see the Son of Man sitting at the right hand of the Mighty One and coming on the clouds of heaven."*
>
> *Then the high priest tore his clothes and said, "He has spoken blasphemy! Why do we need any more witnesses? Look, now you have heard the blasphemy. What do you think?"*
>
> *"He is worthy of death," they answered.*
>
> *Then they spit in his face and struck him with their fists. Others slapped him and said, "Prophesy to us, Messiah. Who hit you?"*
>
> Matthew 26:63-68

From the Romans' point of view, Jesus was a potential subversive threat to their control over Judea. In Jerusalem, the spirit of revolution ran hot during those times as many wanted to overthrow Rome. Jesus had too many followers, and the Empire had no way of knowing if he was peaceful. Plus, he preached that the Kingdom of Heaven was at hand. But the only empire acceptable to Rome was that of Cesar.

When Jesus finally faced Roman oppression face-to-face, what did he do? Did he protest? Did he call for an uprising? No. Jesus gave himself up voluntarily. This was the will of his Father. But still, Jesus did not deny his kingship.

> *Pilate entered the praetorium again and called Jesus, and said to him, "Are you the King of the Jews?"*
>
> *Jesus answered, "My kingship is not of this world; if my kingship were of this world, my servants would fight, that I might not be handed over to the Jews; but my kingship is not from the world."*
>
> *Pilate said to him, "So you are a king?"*
>
> *Jesus answered, "You say that I am a king. For this I was born, and for this I have come into the world, to bear witness to the truth. Everyone who is of the truth hears my voice."*
>
> *Pilate said to him, "What is truth?"*
>
> John 18:33, 36-38

Little did Pilate know that the truth was standing right there in front of him.

So unlike the political-military messiah Cyrus, we have the arrival of the one true Messiah, Jesus Christ. We begin to understand his true, heavenly power. His impact continues to this day – and it's more relevant than ever.

What might the world look like if Jesus' servants did stand up and "fight"? What would happen if we placed all our efforts into directly helping someone in need? What if we stopped pouring money into political causes and used it to help someone we know personally? What if we marched into places of poverty to find out exactly how to help with our feet on the ground? What if our campaigns focused on finding lonely people who need company? What might the result look like? It might look like the Kingdom of Heaven.

Maybe this would unmask the corruption of the rulers. Maybe it would reveal our own selfish tendencies. Jesus was stripped naked to fully expose the deep injustice of this world. He was arrested as a poor, oppressed, and humiliated man.

Jesus is his own political statement. And he is the most serious threat to any "system" ever. And so, a crown of thorns was placed on the head of the true Messiah, the King of kings, Lord of lords. And from there the hidden treasures of his kingship, the true power of God, began to be revealed.

Chapter 24: Limitless

When you reach a hard limit, what do you do? Do you get angry? Do you feel hopeless? Maybe your frustration drives you into a corner. You might get apathetic, or you end up frozen in your tracks.

Hard limits are especially difficult to accept when your expectations are high. You might be waiting for a financial blessing. You might be looking for a new job or counting on an opportunity. Or maybe you belong to a workplace or group, and you feel held back or constrained. Maybe you feel like you can't express your full potential.

Perhaps you've been hoping for a relationship to get better. Or someone you care for has been lost for a long time, and you wish they would change. Or maybe you wish you could change.

And here – in the most important areas of your life – you might come smack up against a brick wall. There is no way over or around it. It will not move or be broken down. And you know it.

Jesus' followers had huge expectations. If he was indeed the Messiah, they knew big changes were coming. And the people of Israel began to have hope. They certainly remembered how King Cyrus freed the people to return to Jerusalem. So if Jesus was the true Messiah, then liberation from Rome's oppression was imminent, wasn't it?

It turns out that the High Priest Caiaphas presided over Jesus' trial in the Sanhedrin. Caiaphas belonged to the most powerful priestly family in Judea, and they were religious aristocrats. The Roman-Jewish historian Josephus wrote that Caiaphas' father-in-law, Ananias, "was a great hoarder of money". Some older, less influential priests even died of starvation since the High Priest's family extorted money from them.

Caiaphas was also on good terms with the Roman prefect Pontius Pilate. They may have even lived in the same prestigious neighborhood, or at least nearby. Pilate represented the unstoppable force of the Roman Empire that was still ascending during Jesus' time. At its height, the Empire ruled over up to a quarter of the world's population.

The full weight of religious corruption – combined with inhuman systematic control – came crashing down on Jesus that terrible day. Forever crushing the liberty of the innocent, these forces conspired to put the Son of Man to death.

There was no way the ruling religious aristocracy and cold-blooded Roman Empire were going to let a semi-homeless, rabble-rousing preacher get away with giving people hope in anything other than the status quo. And the forces succeeded in the most violent and humiliating way. It was an utter defeat for the Jesus movement.

Jesus was arrested and found guilty by a rigged trial. He was whipped and beaten according to the brutal custom for prisoners during the Roman age. They mocked him and spat upon him. And the sacred blood of Christ flowed like a river from his fresh wounds.

During Passover, there was a custom that the Romans would release a prisoner as a gesture of goodwill. Surely it would be Jesus, wouldn't it? But no, the crowd shouted for Barabbas, a notorious bandit, to be set free instead. And so Jesus' fate was sealed; he was sentenced to death. The disciples' hopes and dreams smacked into a brick wall. There was no way over or around it. It could not be moved or broken down. And they knew it.

The Roman soldiers forced Jesus to carry his cross as they drove him forward with the whip. Bleeding, bruised, and exhausted, he eventually reached Golgotha, the place of the Skull. There, they crucified Jesus. They hammered nails through his hands and feet. And the blood of the Son of God soaked the earth. He had reached the hardest limit of all. There was nothing left for Jesus to do. Or was there?

The historic, prophetic, and socio-political contexts of Jesus' Passion, all give us lessons to learn. They give us the necessary perspective of what he was up against. We also may feel threatened by similar forces in our modern age. We might feel like things are hopeless at the macro level (think geopolitics, corruption, technology overwhelm, etc.). In our own life situations, we might feel like there's no way out sometimes. Is there nothing left for us to do?

To understand things better, let's zoom into something much more intimate and personal. Let's unearth the hidden treasures that teach us how to remain in communion with God, even at the hardest, most difficult stops in our lives. It won't be easy, but the things of greatest value never are. If we take a serious look at the secrets of the cross, we will encounter heavenly riches.

When King Cyrus came to power, he was given access to something special...

I will give you hidden treasures,
  riches stored in secret places,
so that you may know that I am the Lord,
  the God of Israel, who summons you by name.

Isaiah 45:3

What might these hidden treasures be? Could they have been gold, jewels, and riches that Nebuchadnezzar had plundered from

155

conquered nations? Did the Israelites bury their treasure deep underground during the siege of Jerusalem? I'm not sure, but the message of throwing open the doors, cutting bars of iron, and receiving hidden treasure speaks to me of Jesus' final words before his death.

According to the Gospels, Jesus spoke seven final phrases from the cross, and each one of them contains great spiritual richness. Our most intimate thoughts are frequently expressed at the height of vulnerability and when we deeply trust in the power of God.

Jesus' words surpass any perverted religious or political force that seeks to control us, no matter how powerful. In our intimacy with God, something much stronger takes shape. It's unstoppable, supernatural, and eternal. So here are Jesus' last words from the cross.

Word 1

"Father, forgive them; for they know not what they do."

Luke 23:34

The first word from the cross is a massive miracle. It's a sledgehammer against any temptation of vengeance. Instead of calling down fire from heaven to destroy his killers, Jesus asks for forgiveness for them all. This may be the most radical word that ever came forth from Jesus' lips.

Think about the worst thing anyone ever did to you. Or the worst thing anyone could ever do to anyone. Then think about forgiving them. Even your deepest darkest secrets or worst thoughts are completely forgiven. Nothing can stop God's forgiveness. It has nothing to do with merit but everything to do with love.

I forgive imperfectly. You do too. But Jesus' forgiveness is complete and perfect. Like a raging fire, it burns away all impurity

156

and hate. And this forgiveness is offered to you and me always forever.

Receive this treasure of forgiveness with all your heart. Embrace and cultivate a spirit of forgiveness in your life. Be liberated from the venom of resentment. Be healthy. Be free. Be holy.

Word 2
"Truly, I say to you, today you will be with me in Paradise."

Luke 23:43

Two criminals were crucified along with Jesus, and one of them even mocked him. But the other criminal asked for salvation. Some of us will always choose the path to damnation, even if God's mercy presents itself explicitly.

The criminal who admits his fault is welcomed by the Son of God into Paradise. This treasure reveals to us that up until our last breath, anything is possible. The followers of Christ rest firmly in this hope, even during times of persecution and pain. Even when they see someone lost and troubled, they don't give up hope.

Here, Jesus' word shows us how to stay hopeful. It's the promise of Eternal Life arriving in the nick of time. Take hold of this great treasure of hope and never let it go. Stand firm upon God's goodness and mercy. Do not be afraid to hope against hope.

Word 3
(To Mary) *"Woman, behold, your son!"* (To the beloved disciple) *"Behold, your mother!"*

John 19:26–27

The third Word is all about relationships. They demonstrate Jesus' concern for his mother and for his beloved disciple. From that moment forward, Jesus' mother Mary was entrusted to the care of his disciple. Some Christian traditions interpret this word as declaring Mary's motherhood for all believers. Even at the height of Jesus suffering, he's cultivating relationships.

Be fully aware of your relationships, even when the going gets tough. Never forsake them. We are happy when we receive and give love. Something so basic frequently escapes us. Remember, healthy relationships are the key to happiness. Cherish them especially in hard times.

Word 4

"My God, my God, why hast thou forsaken me?"

Matthew 27:46

With this word, Jesus cries out along with all those who feel abandoned. He does not shield himself from any of it. A beloved friend betrayed him. He was abandoned by his friends when he needed them most. He was falsely accused and condemned. The hurt drove deep into his flesh – and into his heart.

He also took upon himself all our hurt and shame. One can only imagine the agony Jesus felt hanging on the cross. And appearing like this to his Father – the Son covered in undeserved shame and guilt – must have been unbearable. So, Jesus cried out.

When you are at your lowest, remember Jesus' cry. You can even cry out loud if you want to. But in your cry remember, Jesus is there with you through it all. He does not hide from the suffering. He never abandons you. He takes it with you, and he takes from you. He relieves your soul if you trust in him, if you believe.

Word 5

"I thirst."   John 19:28

In this word, Jesus reveals his full humanity. After hours of physical torture, the Lord is exhausted. His body has been pushed to the limit. He's nearly unconscious, and all he can manage to say is *"I thirst."*

This word also brings to mind Jesus' Sermon on the Mount when he said, *"Blessed are those who hunger and thirst for righteousness, for they shall be satisfied"* (Matthew 5:6).

What kind of righteousness does Jesus thirst for? His vision goes far beyond the belief that the use of force keeps us safe and secure. Jesus' justice is where everyone is treated fairly – where neglect, harm, and control have no place. From there, everyone's needs are satisfied. God is not interested in justice by force. If he were, his Son would not have been hung on a cross. While there will be a final judgment, God's focus is clearly on salvation.

Incorporate this thirst into your veins. It might seem utopic, but we must strive for this. Move past your fears and seek to give life rather than prioritizing survival. This is how the followers of Christ make a difference until he comes again. This attitude might even seem otherworldly to some.

See with the eyes of Christ. Seek his heavenly justice where all are invited to the table as sons and daughters of God.

Word 6
"It is finished"   John 19:30

This word signifies Jesus' life coming to an end. He poured his body, heart, and soul into the mission set before him. He did everything he could and held nothing back. This is the word that emphasizes the Lord's faithfulness until the end.

This word also speaks to us of a culminating event in world history and in the history of our salvation. Jesus died for every single sin committed from the beginning of time onward. Nothing escapes this act of forgiveness. By the blood of Christ, we are set free from the debts of our sin. His sacrifice cements the New Covenant into place for all humankind. The price has been paid, in full, by the Son of Man. Jesus says, *"I am the Alpha and the Omega, the first and the last, the beginning and the end."* (Revelation 22:13)

When Jesus proclaims that *"It is finished,"* it means that sin and death no longer have power over you. You are set free in Jesus Christ's all-consuming victory. So pour your body, heart, and soul into a life fully immersed in the New Covenant. Hold nothing back as you inherit the Kingdom of Heaven.

Word 7
"Father, into thy hands I commit my spirit!"   Luke 23:46

With Jesus' final cry from the cross, he returns to the Father. The Father, Son, and Holy Spirit are eternally united in the Trinity. This has always been Jesus' emphasis – his communion with his Father in the Spirit of God. He knew that all he was, all he was meant to be, and all he could do for others depended on this relationship.

This word is also a declaration of surrender. The entire essence of the Son rests upon and returns to the loving arms of the Father. Even upon facing the inevitability of death, Jesus' trust in his Father is complete.

In this treasured word, Jesus shows you the way. From the moment you are born, and from the moment you accept the Lord into your heart, your destination is unity with our Father in heaven. This doesn't mean you focus on death. Rather, it means you know deep inside that death is not the end of your story.

The result is complete confidence, living 100% in the present, as you hold a promise for an eternal future. Being in sync with God means you trust and surrender to him since you know he provides you with everything your soul desires.

. . . .

Did you see it? Did you see the limitless power of God even in the presence of a hard stop? While nailed to the cross, Jesus shows us immense possibilities. During the crucifixion, his communion with God continues and even thrives showering us with heavenly treasures.

160

From the cross, in the final minutes of his life, Jesus forgave. He offered eternal life. He cultivated relationships. From the cross, Jesus revealed his humanity, and he thirsted for justice. He established the New Covenant once and for all, and he showed us the way to the Father. Even hanging on the cross, for Jesus there were no limits.

Not even the weight of a brutal world empire, entrenched religious corruption, and the harsh reality of execution could stop God's Spirit from working through his Son. When you enter this relationship with all your heart, all your strength, and all your soul – anything is possible. And even the dead can return to life.

Chapter 25: The darkest night

Jesus' crucifixion was absolute. Nothing could have been more shocking and disheartening for his followers than to see their Master's life end in such a tragic way.

Before that day on Calvary, the time the disciples spent with Jesus was filled with hope, joy, and anticipation. And then, he was gone. The night after Jesus' death was a horrible dark moment for his disciples.

Sooner or later, we all go through our own dark nights. During times of loss or difficulty, we might feel God is far away from us or absent. We might even face deep doubts about his existence.

Is it possible that these experiences can somehow bring our faith into sharper focus? Can those dark nights somehow purify our souls?

What follows next is a meditation on what Jesus' disciples might have experienced after his death. Thoughts like this may have gone through their heads after losing their beloved Lord. Let's listen.

. . . .

So, it's over then. Everything I counted on and hoped for. Lost. Forever.

Is this the end?
The death of my Lord and nothing in return. Can anything be worth it now that you are gone?

In my emptiness and suffering, can any meaning be found?

You are one with God. You said you were, and I believed you. Is God dead then now? Or am I dead to God?

Your teachings, your testimony – were they not enough for me? I wish they were. But without you – YOU – I am lost. That which gave life to the Word is now gone. The person of Christ is gone from me.

The deepest part of me suffers. My core. My deepest secrets and pain. My shame and insecurities. I have nowhere to find rest for any of that now. I wander in the wilderness.

I saw the hurt and pain all around me and in the world... and none of it made any sense, until you explained to me. You are my soul's desire.

But now, God is gone. And all I have is sorrow.

Will I continue to strive, nevertheless? Can I still hope against hope? What will life be like now that you are gone? A lifeless life.

Can anything, anyone replace you?

Seeing you, touching you, the tone of your voice and your warm embrace, you look into my eyes and peer into my soul... you know me. All that is gone now.

What holds me together if it is not you? What happens to me now that I cannot be with you?

Nothing else matters now that you are gone. If you are in my mind, are you still in my heart?

O my Lord, what did you intend for me in all this bitterness and pain?

When even you are stripped away from me, what will become of my faith?

What will become of me?

. . . .

In the 16th century, the Spanish mystic, St. John of the Cross wrote about the Dark Night of the Soul. These "dark nights" can occur when someone goes through an intense crisis of faith. Other dark nights can appear during a difficult or painful life event. Sometimes there might be an overlap, as a sudden loss or painful experience can lead to a crisis of faith. During these moments, we can identify with what Jesus' followers might have felt after his death.

When you lose someone close to you, the entire world seems lifeless and without color. When you are going through a tough time, nothing interests you anymore. At first you might feel numb. Then, a deep anguish can set in, and you feel in your bones. You feel it in your body, heart, and soul.

At the mystical or philosophical level, this leads to questions like: what really matters to me, deep down inside? What things define my existence and my joy?

To explore things a bit more, think about this scenario. Let's say you won an all-expense paid trip for two to a beautiful, exotic island. You're excited to make the trip. You imagine sitting on the beach and relaxing with someone you love. Delicious food will be served, and your favorite activities are arranged. Gorgeous sunsets and pleasant evenings are inevitable. You anticipate enjoying a slice of paradise.

Finally, the date of the trip is just around the corner. But the day before your departure, someone close to you gets very sick. Or maybe they even die. What happens then to your thoughts about the island trip? It's the same trip, but your perspective has completely changed. The trip isn't important anymore compared to your worry or sadness.

Jesus' disciples were inspired to follow their leader. They believed in the mission he gave them to share the Good News of the Kingdom of Heaven. They were filled with enthusiasm and bursting with anticipation. But then Jesus got arrested, and they executed him. What now?

Regarding moments like this, St. John of the Cross discovered an unexpected secret: a crisis of faith is an opportunity. How does this happen? Think about it like this. If everything superficial – like a trip to an exotic island – is stripped away, what are you left with? What do you rest upon? If worldly pleasures no longer excite you, what then? Perhaps all you have left is your faith. But what happens if even your faith gets shaken to the core?

All this calls to mind a process of purification. It's where the pleasures of this world no longer drive you. You're not obsessed with food, travel, or entertainment. You're not looking for the next great experience or achievement in life. Nothing matters to you except your communion with God.

But then, even God may seem distant. And you're left with… nothing. But maybe it's not really nothing. Maybe instead, some of your beliefs about faith and salvation were mixed with things that have nothing to do with the truth of God's Spirit.

Perhaps you were confusing material and emotional desires with what your soul truly needs. It could have been social ties or a feeling of self-confidence that nourished you. It might have been the desire to be free of painful memories or a need to be accepted by others. Many things can intermingle with the actual Spirit of truth. But if these desires contain a hidden selfishness, denial, or pride, then it's a problem.

As I write this, I wonder to myself, how much do I truly seek God in purity and faith? What part of me yearns for things that really don't matter that much? I like vacations. I enjoy good food and good company. I have hopes and dreams for my family and friends. Are these bad things? Of course not.

The more important question might be this: are worldly pleasures, objectives, and activities somehow occupying a place in my heart that isn't healthy? Time will tell. Prayer and meditation can reveal it to us. But if any desire gets in the way of our relationship with Jesus, then a purification is required.

In some cases, purification only happens in the dark night – in moments of crisis or loss. Sometimes what really matters becomes crystal clear to you during moments of loss and pain. While you might experience confusion, helplessness, apathy, and even a sense of God's absence at first – if you continue and persevere, something more pure will take root in your heart.

Does it mean you should go live in a cave to get away from it all? Do you have to give up everything and become homeless? Do you have to become a nun, monk, or hermit? Not necessarily, but you can become more holy. And this is worth striving for with all your heart, mind, and soul.

Then, when you look upon the sunset from anywhere, the colors are more vibrant and alive. You see God in all creation, and it fills you with a deep sense of reverence and awe. And when you embrace that special person in your arms, a more powerful bond of trust and faithfulness comes to life.

In Jesus' absence, the disciples certainly realized how much they needed him. And this eventually led them to understand even more deeply the value of his teachings and way of life.

Even if we are living with something painful, our joy cannot be removed if we push forward and trust, despite our doubt and suffering. And I'm not talking about the emotion of happiness, which can come and go. Instead, we can strive to understand and achieve something more profound and mysterious.

When we strip away those superficial, earthly desires, then all that is heavenly and eternal can shine all the brighter even in the dark night of the soul.

. . . .

We are treated as impostors, and yet are true; as unknown, and yet well known; as dying, and behold we live; as punished, and yet not killed; as sorrowful, yet always rejoicing; as poor, yet making many rich; as having nothing, and yet possessing everything.

2 Corinthians 6:8-10

Chapter 26: A bright new dawn

What would being in sync with God 100% of the time look like? Is this even possible? How close can we get to living in tune with our Creator all the time?

Now I haven't achieved this, not even close. But I can picture what it might look like. I think we've all had glimpses of it. I imagine being in tune with God all the time looks something like this...

You open your eyes in the morning and sing praises to God, out loud or with your innermost voice. You greet the day giving thanks to the Lord as the sun shines upon your face. Your early coffee or tea-time is prayerful. And as the morning unfolds, you converse naturally with God to organize your day. Your dialog with him flows freely throughout the morning, afternoon, and evening. Every breath, every word, every motion is full of grace.

In sync with God, you fully grasp the macro context of the world, without losing sight of the little things, like remembering a birthday or anniversary – or remembering to call upon a sick friend. Prudence is your guide as you prepare for things beforehand. Critical events and moments in your life are saturated with anticipatory prayer.

Your life flows seamlessly. It seems like you show up right on time, even if you're running a bit late. And when the turbulence of life swells up, you ride it out, surfing with the rhythm of the Spirit. If the enemy appears, trying to frighten you or seduce you with his lies, you cast the devil out with the hand of God upon you and the name of Jesus on your lips.

And all around you, within you, and from you there is peace. This peace flows from the wounds you have suffered along the way, and some of the scars are visible, others secret. The cuts and bruises are now healed, with the overlying skin soft and smooth. And from the wounds of life, now healed forever, the peace of God flows like a river.

What does being in sync with God all the time look like? I think it looks like the Resurrection.

The Book of Matthew (28:1-10) tells us something incredible happened early on Sunday, the third day after Jesus' crucifixion. Mary Magdalene and "the other Mary" went to visit Jesus' tomb, and upon their arrival there was a great earthquake. Suddenly, an angel of the Lord descended from heaven and rolled back the heavy stone covering the tomb. The angel looked like lightning, his clothing white as snow. And at the sight of him, the tombs' guards trembled in fear and "became like dead men."

Then the angel said to the women, *"Do not be afraid; for I know that you seek Jesus who was crucified. He is not here; for he has risen, as he said. Come, see the place where he lay. Then go quickly and tell his disciples that he has risen from the dead, and behold, he is going before you to Galilee; there you will see him. Lo, I have told you."*

So they departed quickly from the tomb with fear and great joy and ran to tell his disciples. And behold, Jesus met them and said, *"Hail!"* The women fell to his feet and worshiped him. Then Jesus said to them, *"Do not be afraid; go and tell my brethren to go to Galilee, and there they will see me."*

The Resurrection of Jesus Christ is the single most important event in all human history. Even though many Christians might believe this (or say they believe), we sometimes sweep it under the rug. Maybe we feel awkward talking about it or even thinking about it. Perhaps we mention it in passing then quickly move onto the next subject. Or maybe we decide it's something spiritual or metaphorical, but not really real.

Instead of the Resurrection, we might focus on doing good deeds and being charitable. Or we might spend our energy tangled up in culture wars. But being a true follower of Christ doesn't only depend on doing good or fighting for a cause. Instead, a true Christian believes in Jesus' identity and his teachings. We believe he rose from the dead and is living now but not in a symbolic way. We believe he rose from the dead, alive, as a resurrected human being, able to be seen and touched. And from that belief, from a solid faith, all good things follow.

Is it easy to believe that a human being rose from the dead? Let's be honest. The Resurrection isn't something easy to believe in at all. But our faith depends on it. Any chance we might have to be in true harmony with God hinges on the belief that Jesus rose from the dead.

> *If you confess with your lips that Jesus is Lord and believe in your heart that God raised him from the dead, you will be saved.*

> Romans 10:9

Some might say this type of thinking is too narrow. They might say you don't have to believe in the Resurrection. They say that belief in Jesus' teachings and example are enough. But I think it might be the exact opposite.

I believe Jesus' teachings and example alone aren't enough, and they may even limit us on their own. We can get caught up in interpretations and analysis. Our heads can get in the way.

170

Theological arguments and debates have literally lasted for centuries. But when we come to believe that Jesus truly rose from the dead, an entire universe of new possibilities opens up to us.

Yes, we might agree with Jesus' command to help the poor. We may embrace the importance of forgiveness. We might accept that service, kindness, and humility are essential for our world to become a better place. But do we really believe that a man came back to life from the dead? If so, how does it make a difference to us in real-world terms?

If God is love as he says he is, doesn't it make sense that he would send his Son? Doesn't it make sense that he would send a Savior who fully revealed to us the depths of humility, faithfulness, courage, and innocence?

It makes complete sense that God's Son would give us the wisdom of his teachings and perform miracles to prove his authority. And it makes sense that the story of Jesus' life would be amazing, painful, joyful, and sometimes hard to understand, just like ours.

God revealed all his power and glory to us in the most profound, and human, way possible. He didn't come down to entertain us with some kind of cosmic fireworks. None of that would have changed our hardened hearts. Instead, the proof would have to be in the example of a life and love so strong that it even continued beyond death.

The disciples saw the resurrected Jesus with their own eyes. They ate with him and touched his glorified body. He wasn't a zombie or a walking dead. They saw Jesus fully alive, and their encounter with him transformed their lives and changed human history forever.

A small rag tag group of followers found the courage and conviction to announce the Good News, even in the face of ridicule and great danger. And although Jesus' teachings were essential to their message, the core principle from that point forward was the Resurrection of Jesus Christ. With his

Resurrection, Jesus' teachings were charged with something beyond concepts alone. Something supernatural had taken place. Everything else now came alive with the truth of the risen Lord.

I must admit I struggle with my doubts about the Resurrection. There's no reason to hide this fact. When my "rational" mind takes over, I begin to doubt. But over the years, I've discovered something that helps me with this unavoidable element of Christendom. My belief in the Resurrection of Jesus Christ isn't static. Belief evolves. It lives and grows in stages.

There's much more to it than Jesus appearing in the flesh like a rabbit pulled out of a hat. Its meaning reaches far beyond a mere historical event. And the deeper I penetrate into this miracle, and the more I explore it, the closer I get to God. Or maybe a better way to say it is like this: As my faith in the Resurrection gets stronger, the falsehoods in my life get weaker.

Jesus resurrected casts out all those lies that have hurt you over the years. He casts out your insecurities that cause you to react in harmful ways. He casts out the lie that says you, or anyone else, can't change for the better. He casts out the complex rationalizations you make for cutting corners or for doing things you know aren't healthy.

The resurrected Christ casts out the notion that power and control are acceptable ways to get what we want. And this flies in the face of the ruling powers of today's world, the same way it did over 2000 years ago. It flies in the face of the drug dealers, the arms dealers, and any authority that chooses coercion and deceit to rule over people.

But most of all, the risen Jesus casts out fear, since in the Resurrection we discover the full manifestation of God's love.

There is no fear in love, but perfect love casts out fear.

1 John 4:18

God's perfect love is creative, regenerative, and all-powerful. It cannot be stopped, not even by death. All the powers of this world and all the demons of hell cannot stop God's love. Jesus rose from the dead to prove this.

It is the confirmation of all that Jesus taught, said, and did – especially what he did for us on the cross. The Resurrection is revolutionary, which means it liberates us. Even when facing our own natural fear of death, in the Resurrection, we soar free.

The Resurrection defeats what this world tries to sell us, the lie that we need more and more – but it's hard to see sometimes. After the Resurrection, Jesus was sometimes hard to see too. Some of his disciples didn't recognize him at first. They were too tangled up in their sorrow or self-pity, and their hearts were closed. But eventually they saw him and began to see things clearly.

God's astounding, universal power is revealed to us in the most surprising way. The ultimate power, which leads to eternal life, only occurs with humility and self-sacrifice which is totally opposite from what the world teaches us about power. And for this, Jesus Christ is the King of kings and Lord of lords. He is worthy of all thanks and praise. He came to serve us and save us. He died out of love for us. And he rose on the third day to offer us eternal life.

The Resurrection changes you biologically. When you are less stressed and when you are at peace, your body works better and heals faster. You are inspired to care for yourself as you know God exists and he loves you dearly.

Jesus rising changes you spiritually, as your spirit is now given full communication with the Spirit of God. You open up to his guidance. Your spiritual ear tunes into what God's Word says directly to your heart.

The Resurrection changes your life direction. Instead of chasing things that don't bring you true happiness, you clearly grasp what's really important. This doesn't mean settling for less.

Instead, it means reaping all the abundant joy of heaven for your life here and now.

And the Resurrection changes your destiny, for you embark on an amazing journey with your final destination as heaven – forever and for real.

Somewhere, in the deepest, innermost place of your soul, something indestructible exists. And this place yearns to be with God forever. The Resurrection makes this real, makes it possible, and makes it known to you for all eternity.

Chapter 27: Behind closed doors

Have you ever bumped into someone you know that you haven't seen for a long time? I'm sure you have, but maybe you didn't recognize the person at first. It could be they lost or gained weight. Or maybe their hair turned gray or started to thin on top. They might have some new wrinkles that made it hard to recognize them at first.

Did something like this happen to Jesus' disciples after they saw him resurrected? On several occasions, the scriptures say that his followers didn't recognize him right away after he had risen. Why did this happen?

Jesus never lived a life of luxury. He spent countless hours teaching, preaching, and healing. Much of his time was spent walking long distances from town to town. Many times, he didn't have a comfortable place to rest. The activity and stress of life must have left its mark on Jesus' physical appearance, just like anybody else.

Jesus probably looked like any other 30-something first-century Galilean man. In fact, his physical appearance might not have attracted any attention at all. The prophet Isaiah tells us this.

He had no beauty or majesty to attract us to him, nothing in his appearance that we should desire him.

Isaiah 53:2

Then came his Passion. The anguish during Jesus' prayer in Gethsemane caused him to sweat blood. The hours leading up to his death changed his appearance dramatically. He was beaten and bruised, possibly beyond recognition.

So when the Spirit of God resurrected Jesus, what did he look like? Did he look younger, maybe like a 20-something Galilean? Did Jesus reappear looking like he did on his best day of his life before his death? Nobody knows for sure, but his appearance was certainly different.

He wasn't a spirit or ghost. Light didn't shine from his body, and he didn't look like a zombie either. It's quite possible the resurrected Lord looked like an average human being. According to the Gospel of Luke (24:13-35), two of his followers interacted with the resurrected Jesus for hours on the road to Emmaus. And they didn't realize it was him until much later when he broke bread with them.

After his resurrection, Jesus appeared multiple times to his disciples, and frequently, they did not recognize him at first. Apparently, nothing special stood out about him... well, almost nothing.

No matter what Jesus looked like, we do know one thing for sure. Five distinct marks remained on his resurrected body left over from his life before his death. These marks were the nail prints on his hands and feet, and the wound on his side where he was pierced by a Roman soldier's lance.

These are the wounds Jesus suffered on the cross. They remain visible for all eternity, and these wounds contain great treasures. The key to discovering them is found in the Gospels. But you have to look carefully to spot the hidden treasure.

In the Book of John, we find the Lord's disciples hiding in fear on the night of his resurrection. Their leader had been executed, and nothing was certain now. Would they be arrested next? Should they run away? What might happen to them? And suddenly – amid all the doubt and fear – Jesus somehow passes through a closed door and appears to his followers.

Jesus came and stood among them and said to them, "Peace be with you." When he had said this, he showed them his hands and his side. Then the disciples were glad when they saw the Lord. Jesus said to them again, "Peace be with you. As the Father has sent me, even so I send you." And when he had said this, he breathed on them, and said to them, "Receive the Holy Spirit.

John 20:19-22

Did you see it? Did you see the heavenly treasure found in Jesus' wounds? He revealed it clearly to his disciples, and it is revealed to us in the scriptures. At that moment, when he appears to them, Jesus offers his peace twice. And during this offering of peace, he shows them his hands and his side. He shows them his wounds to confirm his identity. He shows them to remind them of what happened and why.

Jesus doesn't try to erase the past. He doesn't pretend like nothing happened. He was betrayed. He was denied. Despite being innocent, Jesus was condemned to death.

The nail and spear marks left a permanent testimony about what Jesus went through, died for, and rose for. But he didn't harbor resentment or seek vengeance, not at all. Instead, he did it all out of love. Then in his final victory over death, he shows us his wounds and offers us his peace.

Think about it this way. How have your own life wounds defined your history? All of us have experiences we would like to forget. But no matter how hard you try, they stick with you. They linger in your memory, and feelings about them can return with an unexpected intensity.

These memories might make you feel sad or ashamed. Or maybe they make you feel angry. And maybe you would do anything to erase those bad experiences from your past, but you know you can't. Those events are a permanent mark on your history, and no matter who's to blame, it hurts. And the pain can make you think or react in ways that make life hard for you.

Undoubtedly, time helps soothe the pain, but it never heals it completely, at least not for me, not for my deepest wounds, not for my worst mistakes. Maybe it's only a handful of events, but they remain etched in your heart and mind.

Seeking treatment for these things can be helpful. Talking to a counselor or psychologist can do wonders for understanding how to deal with past trauma or deep guilt. But I believe there's an innermost place in all of us where nobody can reach... well, almost nobody.

In my heart of hearts all the human help in the world isn't enough. But what about the innocent One who washes the feet of sinners? My heart of hearts cannot resist his humility. What about the One who gives me all of his heart without limits, the One that carries his wounds with him for all eternity to remind me of his eternal love? That's who can heal my innermost hurt. He's the only One I can trust completely.

It's not that nobody else can help me. It's not that nobody else cares. But in that secret place, only Christ can bring true healing. Everyone is imperfect, so I can't expect them to provide me with the deep healing I desperately need. In fact, it wouldn't be fair to place such an expectation on anyone. Only God can reach deep inside to heal the innermost part of the soul. The prophet Isaiah says it like this:

But he was pierced for our transgressions,
  he was crushed for our iniquities;
the punishment that brought us peace was on him,
  and by his wounds we are healed.

Isaiah 53:5

178

If we combine this passage with the one earlier, where Jesus offers his peace and shows us his wounds, things become clearer. Our most painful moments are frequently the result of some kind of transgression. You did something or someone did something to you. Or maybe it was a tragic loss.

Jesus takes it all with him to the cross. But he didn't stay dead. Instead, he rose from the dead. And the marks from the nails and the tip of the lance remain on his body. But now, the wounds don't bleed and don't sting anymore. Instead, they are sealed and healed forever.

Can our wounds be the same? Maybe you'll never forget about them completely. But you can rise above them, even if you've been seriously hurt or did something seriously wrong. Denial never works. Endless blame and shame are intolerable. Instead, the Resurrection shows us a more excellent way.

Jesus doesn't offer you amnesia or an escape from reality. Instead, he gives you his peace – the peace produced by his wounds that were suffered out of love. And Jesus' love is all powerful and pure. It's a universe-creating level of love. And for some wounds, only that level of healing will do the job.

It's a love beyond all measure that somehow makes you whole again, even though you still carry your scars. His peace pours out from his wounds, visible for all eternity. They remind us constantly who he is and how much he loves us.

So rather than banging your head against a wall asking why things had to happen, instead of living through repeated bouts of anguish, you finally accept your story. You are at peace with your history. For many, this is nothing less than a miracle, and that's why it can only come from God.

Now, even though you don't forget, you can move forward. You are transformed and live courageously. You choose the path of life that leads to eternal life. You rise with Christ. And in some

179

strange, wonderous way, your deep wounds let you identify with the Son of God, because he identifies with you.

Now you are wiser and more kind as you understand what it means to live with hurt. And the deeper the wound, the deeper the understanding. In the name of love, you move past the pain and shame as you are certain you are loved beyond all measure.

Christ's wounds heal you. They give you everlasting peace. They assure your peace with your Creator. And this lets you live and love unlike ever before.

Conclusion: Expect the unexpected

Many times, while writing this book, I said it was a sort of a spiritual experiment. And even now, as we near the end, I'm still discovering new things. I'm thankful and feel God has been accompanying us along the way. I still have a lot to flesh out, day by day, but I feel like it was a good start. You might be thinking, 'a good start'? How can the end of a book be the beginning?

At the time of writing this final chapter, it's almost Christmas. Every year we return to the beginning as we wait in joyful hope for the coming of our Savior Jesus Christ. But I also see a fragmented world. I see many challenges unlike any other time in history. There's so much going on, and so much information presented to us. It's nearly impossible to make sense of things sometimes.

I believe this is part of the reason why so many people feel anxious and depressed these days. Some turn to fanaticism and ideology to try to navigate it all. Others just throw up their hands and give up. We desperately need something solid we can rely on to guide us through these uncertain times.

The events that will take shape over the next several years will be world changing. The balances of power are shifting and unstable. Technology continues to advance at exponential rates. Nobody knows what kind of impact artificial intelligence will have on humanity. Some say it will give rise to another intelligent species, which would be unlike anything we've ever seen before. Meanwhile, any notion of world peace seems farther away than ever.

The world is coming to grips with an existential crisis of massive proportions. And it's no surprise that conversations about God have made their way back into the mainstream. Not too long ago, the secular world made it taboo to talk about things like faith in God. Now, as we face tremendous challenges, a deep yearning for meaning cannot be silenced.

> *"We know that the whole creation has been groaning in travail together until now."*

Romans 8:22

And so, let's think about Christmas. How do we celebrate now? In our turbulent, fast paced world is there any room for simplicity? Is there any room for joy? I'm not talking about mere happiness. Special moments and events can make us happy, like the birth of a child. But what about the joy of the soul? What about the deep joy that gives us perspective when times are good? And what about the lasting joy that lifts us up when times aren't so good?

This kind of joy must come from God. It must come from Spirit and Truth. And yes, perhaps we can discover this kind of joy in the birth of a child. As we have seen in previous chapters, for the followers of Jesus, the greatest truth is his Resurrection. It's there where we find our greatest joy as well.

The risen Christ is the embodiment of every key aspect of our relationship with God. It's the prophecy, the promise, and the miracle. It's the power of our covenant with our Creator. It is the *"assurance of things hoped for, the conviction of things not seen"* (Hebrews 11:1). It is the essence of our faith.

For the deepest questions that plague us, in the Resurrection, you can drill down and reach a concrete answer. The other option is to just not think about it. But what happens if we try to live oblivious to what our souls cry out for? At what cost do we ignore the cry of our soul? And what is the reward when our soul receives what it desires most?

In our certainty in the Rock that is the risen Christ, we find joy. And despite the world's trials and challenges, despite the uncertain future, and during our hardest questions, our joy actually deepens. It comes into sharper focus as it contrasts against the confusion of modern times.

Our faith becomes clearer, stronger, and more real than ever. It shines all the brighter, even in the darkest night. In a strange way it's a secret. You have no idea what it's about until you experience it. The joy of the sons and daughters of God is a monumental secret, but it's there for all the world to receive.

And this joy of the soul, by nature expands and grows stronger. It yearns to share itself with others. And when joy thrives, even in the hardest situations, it's totally unexpected – just like the birth of a Savior in a manger. Just like the birth of a King in a stable. Just like the birth of the Son of God to a Virgin.

While writing this book, I've often talked about value. The most valuable things in life require the most dedication and care. Family, friends, community, education, work, and even faith. These are the things of highest value. And a newborn child who is the Savior of the world? How much value do we find there for our lives? The scriptures give us a clue…

> *When they saw the star, they rejoiced exceedingly with great joy; and going into the house they saw the child with Mary, his mother, and they fell down and worshiped him. Then,*

opening their treasures, they offered him gifts, gold and frankincense and myrrh.

Matthew 2:10-11

They fell down and worshiped him, it says. They offered him gifts.

For where your treasure is, there will your heart be also.

Matthew 6:21

Years later, when Jesus began his public ministry, he went to the synagogue at Nazareth. He stood up to read from the book of the prophet Isaiah. He opened the book and found the place where it was written:

"The Spirit of the Lord is upon me,
because he has anointed me to preach good news to the poor.
He has sent me to proclaim release to the captives
and recovering of sight to the blind,
to set at liberty those who are oppressed,
to proclaim the acceptable year of the Lord."

Luke 4:18-19

Then Jesus closed the book and sat down. All the eyes of those in the synagogue were fixed on him. And Jesus said to them, *"Today this scripture has been fulfilled in your hearing."*

Did you hear that? Today is the day. Now is the time. Now is the time to receive the Good News. Now is the time to enjoy your freedom as a child of God. Today is the day to see with clear eyes the path set before you. And now is the time to be liberated from the oppression of all that holds you back from growing as a human being. God's mighty hand will guide you and set you free.

Don't put it off any longer! Strive now to get in sync with God. It's simple, but it does require effort. Read your Bible. Go to church. Pray. Nothing at all can stop you... except yourself. God will help you. And what's the real secret? God waits for you, always. He waits for you to come closer to him. He doesn't force you. He lets you take all the time you need. It depends on your decision. He lets you. So let him. Let him in and let him be God in your life.

In this book we have explored the scriptures, from Eden to Moses to Elias to John the Baptist, we chewed upon the reasoning behind it all. We've looked at the proposal of faith from perspectives of the head and of the heart. And we've examined our own histories that are full of trials, hope, and joy.

Is it even possible to summarize what it means to be in tune with God? I think there might be a way. We know God is love. And if you know Jesus, you know he loves you infinitely. The evidence is indisputable. So what's your response?

You love God back.

You love him truly and deeply.

And when you love someone, you pay attention to them. You listen to them. They are your priority. And it pleases you to please them.

Loving someone is so good for you.

If you truly explore, understand, and receive God's love, the only response is to love him in return. And in your love for him, you will be in communion with him.

And so, you wait in joyful hope, for the *second* coming of our Savior, our Lord Jesus Christ.

Supplemental content…

Be With Him
Him
Be Like Him

Introduction

What place does prayer hold in your life? Is it something you mumble before meals or when tucking the kids into bed? Or is it something that has transformed you?

We are convinced that we have to do it all. So we set up organizations and campaigns to try to solve all the problems of the world. Meanwhile, our daily personal struggles are fought in solitude.

How many miracles can you attribute to God answering your prayers? One? Five? Ten? Believe it or not, when you embark on a life dedicated to prayer, you will lose count of the miracles and incredible events that begin to happen.

There's a great God just dying to hear you and help you. When you deepen your understanding about who he is, then everything changes. Prayer is an essential part of this process, and that makes it an essential part of life.

This prayer book is written for everyone, even those with a life rich in prayer. You won't find a list of rules telling you how to pray, but you will find a perspective here that you might never have considered.

So come on in, get comfortable, and discover the tremendous joy found in an intimate communion with God.

Chapter One: Early Morning

If I were to offer you one hundred dollars to sit in a chair for thirty minutes every day at six a.m., would you do it? How about for five hundred dollars? A thousand? What value do we place upon our time spent alone with God? Where do we find the time? Think about this:

For where your treasure is, there your heart will be also. (Matthew 6:21)

Your time is valuable. We all have a set amount of time on this earth, and it can't be bought or sold. If we're going to spend our time on any activity, we should be sure that it's worth it. So is prayer worth the time?

When seeking the answer, we should look towards the man whose prayers made a huge impact upon the world. Can we find some inspiration in the example of Jesus Christ?

Throughout the Gospels we find Jesus making time to pray. In all of human history, no other person's time held more value. Still, Jesus set aside time exclusively to be alone with God. In the Gospel of Mark it says:

Very early in the morning, while it was still dark, Jesus got up, left the house and went off to a solitary place, where he prayed. (Mark 1:35)

So here we have Jesus, making prayer his first priority, getting up before dawn to seek the presence of his Father. But why? Couldn't Jesus have done the things he did without prayer? Didn't he know the difference between right and wrong? He was the Son of God after all. Wasn't there a lot of good he could have been doing instead, like healing the sick? Why did he pray so much?

We are creatures of action. Early humans, when hungry, went out and killed an animal to eat. We like to be able to execute a plan. But we are spiritual creatures as well. Perhaps the only thing that sets humans apart from the animals is our desire to seek and know God.

Ironically though, our flesh rejects acts of faith. We want to act instead of being silent and still in God's presence. Modern society tries to crush the Spirit of prayer out of us. It's no wonder that mental illness has become the developed world's number one disease.

But in moments of private communication, we can come into direct and intimate contact with God. Just like Jesus.

Some argue that there are many ways to pray. For example, some say that helping others is a form of prayer. Is this true? Helping others is helping others, and helping is a good thing. But prayer is prayer, and, believe it or not, it's the best thing (Luke 10:42).

I can tell my six-year-old, "Listen son. We're going to spend the whole morning together, just you and me, OK?"

Then I can open up my computer and spend all day working to make money to feed my family while my son plays with his toy cars on the floor next to me. Maybe I'll even donate the money to charity. My son and I are together, and I'm doing something good, right? Sure, but I'm not engaged with my son. What I need to do is close my computer, get on the floor, grab a toy car and play. Vroooooom! It's the same way with God. We need to stop everything and give him our complete attention.

In the field of neurotheology, scientists at some of the world's most prestigious medical institutions have shown that prayer can actually sculpt the brain, giving us a way to change our thought patterns. Here science confirms faith. This is something Jesus already knew and taught over 2000 years ago. However, Jesus digs deeper than what can be demonstrated in scientific studies alone. Prayer is a life changing and life-giving force. Jesus desires to change our hearts, not just our heads.

If a king or a president planned to come visit you at home, would you schedule some other activity for the same time? Of course not. There is no greater King than Jesus Christ. So give him the time and attention he deserves.

I don't like sugar coated messages because many times you end up swallowing a hidden, poisonous core. The rest of this book will demand much from you. When I entered medical school, my goal was to obtain a real medical license. If someone tried to sell me a fake one, I would have turned them down. The path will be rocky and lined with thorns, but it leads to glory.

Prayer does not promise a life full of butterflies and roses; it should not anesthetize you spiritually. Instead, prayer promises a life full of the Spirit in communion with our Creator.

Chapter Two: Setting Up Your Prayer Time

We just talked about a king visiting your home. Your prayer time must be exactly that: prayer time. Try to consciously set aside time in your schedule for prayer. This moment should not be compromised. Remember, it's your appointment with the King! So guard this time jealously. It will be your point of spiritual combat (we'll explore this later).

You can start at any time you like, but don't make it something you do in your spare time. Mark it on your calendar. You can start gradually if you like, maybe once or twice a week. This might sound like an exercise plan, because it is. This is a plan for you to get spiritually fit and strong. And your strength comes from coming into contact with the God of life itself.

You want to build up your time spent in prayer. Just like the well-trained athlete, you should get to a point where it's a daily commitment. Don't wait to feel inspired or to pray only in times of great need. Your prayer should be a living, breathing part of your life. When you miss your prayer time, it should feel like you missed a meal. Indeed, in prayer we receive true sustenance.

I hesitate to give exact numbers, but if you invest time, your prayer will be fruitful. Ideally, you should find time (in quality and quantity) nearly every day for communion with God.

You might be thinking, "No way do I have time to dedicate to prayer," but listen. There are many faithful Christians that dedicate thirty minutes, or even an hour, to prayer every day. These are laypersons. They work regular jobs and have a family, which they do not neglect in the least. If anything, their prayer life allows them to cherish their family even more. If we trust in God, he will make the time available for us to comply with all of our responsibilities, including prayer.

On the other hand, there are perhaps millions of Christians that dedicate almost no time to prayer at all. Imagine how the heavens would move if all of them knelt in prayer every day!

How much time do you dedicate to television? To reading the newspaper or books? To using your computer or to hobbies? Are these things more important than your appointment with the King?

Please don't get intimidated. You don't start by praying an hour every day. Try starting with a 15-30 minute prayer session once a week for a month or so. The important thing is to keep this appointment faithfully, then build up gradually.

When you dedicate time to prayer, God helps you to organize your thoughts, which is the key to organizing your life. Instead of being easily distracted, fearful or without direction, you know where to go and when to act. You don't waste time, and you think with clarity.

However, it goes far beyond just having a clear mind. Truths will be revealed to you. Important questions will be answered. You will intervene on behalf of others. You become an active instrument in the expansion of God's Kingdom. You will find forgiveness. And you will forgive.

Prayer time is not time wasted, but time gained.

You can find no greater way to invest your time. So mark it on your schedule and keep the date. Guard your prayer time jealously.
****

KEY CONCEPTS: For where your treasure is, there your heart will be also. (Matthew 6:21)

→ Start with a basic plan: 15-30 minutes, once a week.

→ From the beginning, maintain strict faithfulness to your prayer time.

→ Build up gradually, but always with the vision to increase your time spent in prayer.

→ Time spent in prayer is time gained.

Chapter Three: I don't know how to pray. What do I say?

The loss for words during prayer is very common. First of all, try to remember that your prayer is a dialogue. If we reduce it to a mechanical process, then we might as well play a recording to pray for us.

God wants us to talk to him. And he wants to respond.

First of all, find a quiet and private place to pray. Shut the door, turn off your phone, and make sure you won't be distracted. Remember, one of the secrets to prayer is to pray in secret. At first you might have a million thoughts racing through you mind. So let them race and let them run away. Let your mind unwind in God's presence and don't feel rushed.

If you have never prayed before, or if your experience is limited, you can begin with some simple words of praise. This puts the focus on God. You might begin, for example, with:

Here I am Lord. I am here to praise you and worship you. You are worthy of all thanks and praise. Your name is sacred and holy. Praise to you, oh Lord. (Then go on continuing with similar words of praise and thanksgiving).

Then you can invoke the Holy Spirit:

Oh, Holy Spirit, fill me. Fill this space with your presence. Fill me with your presence, oh Spirit of God. Fill me with your light. Oh, Holy Spirit, fill me, restore me, complete me. (This type of invocation can also be repeated.)

It's important to avoid simply reading or memorizing prayers. These are just examples to help get you started. Let the Spirit guide your words. Let the Spirit show and teach you how to pray effectively.

Some other phrases that can be used are:

…Lord Jesus, I trust in you.

…Take control, Lord.

…Let your will be done, oh Lord.

…Have mercy on me, Lord.

From here there are various ways that you can continue. One of the best ways is to begin talking to God as you would to a close friend. Even though he knows all of your needs, he wants to hear how you express things to him. Let it all out. Tell him your worries, your joys, your fears, your sufferings and ask him to free you and heal you. Ask him to forgive you. Don't forget to thank and praise him throughout this conversational prayer.

All of the prayers described above are a way to help you get closer to God. They are words of praise, thanksgiving, intimacy and trust. These are essential elements for you to move forward in your spiritual development. This spontaneous type of prayer helps you build your relationship with Jesus. Later, we will explore a more complete way to pray, which uses the Our Father as a guide.

****

KEY CONCEPTS: Praise the Lord, my soul; all my inmost being, praise his holy name. (Psalm 103:1)

→ Start your prayer praising God.

→ If you ask for things, ask in Jesus' name.

→ Talk to God as you would to a friend or mentor.

→ The secret to prayer is to pray in secret.

Chapter Four:
Confronting Obstacles
– Spiritual Combat

This topic appears relatively early in this book because it will appear early in your prayer life. You will not want to pray. You'll get sleepy. Or suddenly you'll become very busy with apparently better things to do. Life will tug and pull you away from your time spent with the Lord. Be aware that this will be a constant issue. And when this happens, press on.

This is the spiritual battlefield.

Some may not believe in Satan, but all the misery and atrocity in this world are all the proof I need. The devil never appears to us with horns and a pitchfork. He presents things to us just as he did to Eve – seductive and pleasing to the eyes. He manipulates our desires and fears with great skill and precision. Then we become busybodies, running around, and meanwhile God waits for us patiently.

One of Satan's greatest victories is to get us up off of our knees and send us scurrying after the worries of the world. There we encounter every temptation to separate us from our loved ones and from God's will.

Every single aspect of your life contains a spiritual component. Every crisis, every challenge, every illness, every disturbance and every conflict is being fought on an invisible plane of existence where angels and demons engage in combat. We can only influence this area through prayer. Our prayers wield tremendous power. They are the fuel for miracles and transformations.

Many times, I don't want to pray, and the resistance is nearly palpable. I have to literally force myself to start. I get drowsy, and sometimes I even doze off. But I press on.

"Fight for me Lord," I ask. "Give me strength. I need you. I trust you."

Those prayer sessions often end up being the most intense and end with a great presence of the Holy Spirit. When you push through this breech, you obtain clear insight into your life and God's greater plan for the world.

If you fail to meet your obligations, don't get discouraged. Again, this is exactly what the enemy wants, and he will use every method to prevent you from praying. So put the enemy in his place. Cast evil into the abyss. Send him away from you with these words:

"In the name of Jesus Christ, away from me Satan!"

Then, raise the banner of thanks and praise to our living God.
****

KEY CONCEPTS: For though we live in the world, we do not wage war as the world does. (2 Corinthians 10:3)

→ You will be tempted greatly to skip your prayer time. Don't give in, and don't give up!

→ Spiritual combat is waged on your knees. Victories are later realized in your daily life.

→ Ask the Lord to fight for you and to give you strength.

Chapter Five:
Consulting with God in Prayer

If you are like me, your tendency is to make plans first and ask God later. We want to do it our way then ask God to bless our projects and decisions. Many times, he even gives us clear instructions, and we ignore them.

It might go something like this. I could tell my son one day, "Listen son. We're expecting some important guests this afternoon. Could you do me a favor and straighten up the house while I go buy some refreshments?"

In my absence, my son decides to wash the car. He does a great job, and the vehicle sparkles without a single speck of dust.

"Look Dad!" my son says upon my return, "Look at the car! Doesn't it look great? I did it for you!"

"Yes son, it looks wonderful. But didn't I ask you to straighten up the house?"

This is very typical. I have fallen into this trap too many times. There can be many reasons why we do this. We might be in a hurry. We might be distracted. Or we might be too proud to take the time out to consult with or listen to God. We want all the glory for ourselves.

Instead, our lives must glorify Jesus Christ.

So ask God. Ask him what he wants. It will always be the best for you. It might not please you at the moment, but later you'll understand. When we go to the Lord in prayer and consultation, we receive a promise. Whatever he asks us to do will be blessed! We leave the factory with a divine guarantee. We act in his will. Only in obedience can we mature in our faith. Remember what Jesus said, "Thy will be done."

This process of consultation might take a while, so don't feel hurried. You might have to return and get confirmation. Ask, ask and ask again. Search the Bible as you pray and look for confirmation in God's word. When your prayer and the Word are in line together, then you will feel peace and assurance. This will be all the grace and blessing you need.

Now things might not go exactly as you imagined, even if you consulted with God previously. But he gives us the direction, and he will guide us through.

Don't be afraid to ask for details. You can think in terms of the who, what, where, when, why and how of each consultation. For example, after Saul's death, David consulted with God about what to do (2 Samuel 2:1).

David asked, "Shall I go up to one of the towns of Judah?"

"Go up," the Lord replied.

"Where shall I go?" David said asking for details.

"To Hebron," answered the Lord.

As God commanded, David obeyed and went up to Hebron, and there he was crowned King of Judah and eventually King of Israel. This shows God's willingness to give us specific answers. It might take time, but he will answer. In this way we can know the will of God in our lives.

So go to him and ask about anything. Or even better, ask him about everything. Seek his guidance in all matters, big or small.

Issues about family and money are especially important. Also, your service or ministry to God should come from revelation in consultation. Keep your emotions out of it. Let him put the conviction in your heart. Then you know it's the Spirit acting through you.

****

KEY CONCEPTS: "For I know the plans I have for you," declares the Lord, "plans to prosper you and not to harm you, plans to give you hope and a future. Then you will call on me and come and pray to me, and I will listen to you. You will seek me and find me when you seek me with all your heart." (Jeremiah 29:11-13)

→ Make a habit of consulting with God before taking action.
→ Consultation with God blesses your actions.
→ The process takes time.
→ Don't be afraid to ask for details.
→ Consult with God on all matters, great or small.

Chapter Six: Praying for Others

This type of prayer is called intercession or intercessory prayer. It's a central element to our prayer life. As mentioned previously, prayer is spiritual fuel. Miracles and transformations occur in large part, thanks to our prayers.

There are many reasons that you will pray for others. Physical health and healing are very common motives for intercession. You might ask for God to intervene when a person close to you is undergoing a personal crisis, perhaps in their marriage or at work. Or maybe you hope to see someone break free from their alcohol or drug addiction. I know people that have prayed for a specific person for years, and the person receiving the prayers never even knew about it.

You can pray for whole families, groups, towns, cities and countries. You should pray for political and religious leaders too. In fact, prayers should be offered for the entire world, especially for zones of disaster, famine or war.

Perhaps the most intense and important type of intercession, however, is the prayer for conversion. This is when you pray for someone to accept Jesus Christ as his or her Savior. The reason for the intensity of this prayer is that it requires three powerful ingredients: sincerity, faith and love.

Frequently, parents, for example, pray for their children's well-being, health and prosperity. But they hesitate when it comes to conversion. Deep down, they might be thinking, "Well as long as Jimmy and Jane are happy and healthy, then they don't need Jesus." They might even secretly want to shield their children from the trials that come with being a disciple of Christ. So, if anything, your prayer for conversion must be sincere.

You might be tempted to think that your prayers can't bring someone to Jesus. You might feel that you have to convince the person instead. We must share the Gospel message; this is undeniable, and God's grace is his alone. But prayers are the other cornerstone in the transformation of lives, and you must believe wholeheartedly in this. Jesus said, "Ask and it will be given to you..." (Matthew 7:7). So, if anything, have faith when you pray for conversion.

Finally, intercessory prayer is an expression of love. It shows you love the Father, because you seek his presence and go to him. It shows you love others, because you intercede for them with sincerity and faith. Are you asking for a conversion just so a certain person does not bother you anymore? Do you want them to conform to your will? Do you want the glory of their conversion for yourself? Examine your conscience. What is your motive? If it is not love, then God probably isn't interested. So, if anything, your prayer must be loving.

God uses our prayers to extend his kingdom and to enact his will. Can there be anything more powerful than the will of God? Your prayers make a huge difference on the spiritual level and on the earthly level. If you implement sincerity, faith and love in your intercession, you will enter into the wondrous process of miracles and transformed lives.

We must consider one final point. Many times, intercession is a long, drawn-out process. You might pray for years, even decades and not see any result. Remember though, God says that his "ways are higher than your ways" (Isaiah 55:9). You might not like the wait, but be patient and persevere. Do not give up, and do not give in. Draw on the Spirit for strength. Double your efforts and wait upon the Lord. Love has no limits.

For the revelation awaits an appointed time; it speaks of the end and will not prove false. Though it linger, wait for it; it will certainly come and will not delay. (Habakkuk 2:3)

This verse underscores the one aspect that ties all intercessory prayer activity together: hope.

The power of prayer might be resisted for a time, but it cannot be denied forever.

****

KEY CONCEPTS: And the prayer offered in faith will make the sick person well; the Lord will raise them up. If they have sinned, they will be forgiven. (James 5:15)

→ Intercession is a critical element for God's will to be done.

→ Intercessory prayer can be done for any person, group or nation.

→ The prayer for conversion must be sincere, done in faith and based in love.

→ Hope keeps the intercessory prayer alive.

Chapter Seven: The Cry

There are times when you have reached the end of your rope. Or maybe you are passing through a desert. Or you might find yourself in a den of ravenous wolves. In these types of circumstances, you can rely on one of the most important forms of prayer of all: The Cry.

There are many episodes in the Bible where a person or a group cried out to God for deliverance. While living in bondage in Egypt, the Hebrew slaves cried out to the Lord, and he heard their cry (Exodus, chapters 2 and 3). This crying out moved God and led to one of the most important liberations in history. The nation of Israel was delivered. Passover, the prequel to Easter, was established and the Law was given. It all started with crying out to God.

When facing a large invading army, Jehoshaphat, King of Judah, remembered the Lord´s faithfulness. He reminded his people: "If calamity comes upon us, whether the sword of judgment, or plague or famine, we will stand in your presence before this temple that bears your Name and will cry out to you in our distress, and you will hear us and save us." (2 Chronicles 20:9)

In our lives we all will face some kind of oppression or threat eventually. It can take many different forms, some even life threatening. It might be economic hardship, illness or a great personal struggle.

In these extreme cases you have a most powerful resource: your cry out to God.

Why does God wait for your cry? If he is merciful and kind, why does he wait? Again, we can go back to the example of the Hebrew slaves in Egypt. Their deliverance was of monumental importance in the history of salvation through Jesus Christ. The situations in our individual lives are no different. Our greatest crises are of monumental importance to our personal history of salvation. God always has a bigger and better plan.

This does not mean that everything will turn out exactly as you like. The Israelites ended up wandering around in the desert for 40 years after exiting Egypt, and only the following generation entered into the Promised Land. However, a greater meaning was established in their crying out to God.

When you get to the point where you must truly cry out, there is a huge advance in your walk of faith. You go to him with all your needs and suffering and anguish. You throw yourself at him and at the feet of his mercy. You learn to depend upon his will and his way. Here you find great meaning to your trials because, through communion with God, you seek the most important answers in your life. You are exposed, naked and vulnerable before that which is all powerful.

Sometimes things turn out exactly, or nearly exactly, as you ask. Nearly always, additional unforeseen blessings are heaped on top of it all. After all, he is a good and generous God.

However, the answer is not always in what you are asking for specifically, but instead the answer can be found in the cry itself. God's response is guaranteed. And if your cry is sincere, and if it comes from deep trust, then you enter into a higher level of understanding and grace. Without the bondage there could be no Passover. Without the crucifixion, there could be no resurrection. All things lead back to God for those who put their hope and trust in him. In all things, God works for the good of those who love him (Romans 8:28).

So when the darkness comes and you're not sure; when the enemy is advancing and arrives at your doorstep – cry out. Cry out to the Lord with all your heart, strength and soul. This is the deepest form of prayer. Your Father in heaven always hears your cry.

****

KEY CONCEPTS: The Lord said, "I have indeed seen the misery of my people in Egypt. I have heard them crying out because of their slave drivers, and I am concerned about their suffering." (Exodus 3:7)

→ The heartfelt cry out to God is a cry for deliverance.

→ This cry not only advances your faith, but it also advances God's plan for your life.

→ Always remember the Lord's faithfulness.

Chapter Eight: Group Prayer

One of the pillars of the Christian faith is that following Christ means being part of a community. We should be in communion with Jesus and also with other believers. An obvious extension of this concept is group prayer.

If we look to the Acts of the Apostles, there are many instances where the primitive Church relied on moments of community prayer. Even if it's just with one or two other people, group prayer stimulates your spiritual growth in a unique way. You strengthen others, and you draw strength from them. To worship God with others is one of the most beautiful ways to be a living part of the Body of Christ. God does not want us to be separated and isolated. He wants us to share.

When we pray in a group there is strength in numbers. The prayer is very often intercessory in nature. First of all, we can ask for the needs of the people in the prayer group. We can also, as a group, intercede for others. Group memory means we are less likely to leave out important prayer needs be they global or personal. If a personal crisis is the object of prayer, then the others in the group can provide caring support.

You can look to your local church or parish to join an already established prayer group, or you can start your own. One way to do this is to find at least one or two other people that you trust. Then schedule to get together at least twice a month. Once a week is even better.

The challenges that go along with group prayer are very similar to the challenges that go along with individual prayer. It will seem like suddenly a million distractions and obligations will keep you from getting together. In some ways, God plans this. He wants to test your commitment and develop your character. He does this on an individual as well as a group level. Obviously, you don't want to badger anyone into participating, but it's important to show others that prayer is a top priority in your life. This in itself is a testimony.

I am part of a prayer group that I joined somewhat reluctantly. When I first joined, I thought, "Well, I'll participate for now, but if something more important comes up, then I'll leave the group." But you know what? Nothing is more important.

That's right. Community prayer is as important as individual prayer. Again, we see the example of Jesus and his disciples as well as the example of the early church. Each prayer group constructs their relationship with the Lord in their own very special manner. Many times, concrete projects of charity or solidarity are born out of these prayer groups.

Each person becomes a testimony for the other as the group pushes forward. And when the Lord eventually delivers, it's a strong testimony for the entire group. Faith grows at the individual level and the group level, and the entire Body of Christ is strengthened in the process.

There is a danger to be aware of that can appear in any group. It is best expressed in James 3:16:

For where you have envy and selfish ambition, there you find disorder and every evil practice.

James 3:17-18 also gives us the remedy:

But the wisdom that comes from heaven is first of all pure; then peace-loving, considerate, submissive, full of mercy and good fruit, impartial and sincere. Peacemakers who sow in peace reap a harvest of righteousness.

****

KEY CONCEPTS: They all joined together constantly in prayer, along with the women and Mary the mother of Jesus, and with his brothers. (Acts 1:14)

→ To be a Christian means belonging to a community.

→ Praying with others allows for mutual intercession and edification.

→ Praying with others helps you remember important things to pray for.

→ Beware of jealousy and ambition.

Chapter Nine: Prayer for Married Couples

It was a strange thing. Even though my walk with the Lord has been very involved, it took me years before I began to pray on a regular basis with my wife alone. We prayed together with our children every day, but our prayer time as a married couple took time to appear. I have speculated that the reasons could have been anything from embarrassment to lack of time or just plain absentmindedness. Perhaps negligence was the real reason.

Deep down, however, I know that the enemy was behind it all. They day my wife and I first prayed together – just the two of us – it was a great victory for the Kingdom of God. There's nothing more the devil wants to do than separate us. He wants to separate us from our family, our community, our loved ones and from our Father in heaven. Satan prefers to keep us isolated and anesthetized.

Matrimony is the ultimate union between man and woman. You become one flesh (Genesis 2:24). It's no wonder that the prayer that comes from this union is especially important and powerful. When you intercede as a couple, your two prayers combine into one prayer formed deeply in love.

I believe God pays special attention to this type of prayer, because he knows that behind it is a sacred union and, in many cases, a family. In our experience, the fruit of this prayer is better communication between my wife and me. Our parenting has also become more harmonious. Our children benefit with concrete changes occurring in their lives.

Perhaps the greatest fruit of this prayer is the Lord's cultivation of the love between spouses. God directly ripens, matures and shapes this union when he is praised and worshipped by both at once. Most importantly, your love for God will deepen. This happens both as individuals and as a couple. Each is better able to serve the other, and all of this glorifies Jesus Christ.

So as in other prayer sessions, plan prayer time with your spouse alone. In our lives this is sometimes done on the run, but God prepares each moment if we just listen to him.

Begin just by talking a bit about important things in your life and in your heart. This will help you see what direction your prayer will take.

Listen carefully. Then pray.

Don't be structured about it. Take turns talking to the Lord. Make sure to pray for each other. Pray for your marriage. If you have children, pray for each one by name. Create prayer projects together where you focus the intercession from the two of you. Ask God to show you what plans he has in mind for you as a couple and, if you have been so blessed, as a family.

You will find you end up loving each other on a celestial level. There is no doubt that God's angels sing with great joy upon witnessing this expression of love between husband and wife.

****

KEY CONCEPTS: This is why a man leaves his father and mother and is united to his wife, and they become one flesh. (Genesis 2:24)

→ Prayer between married couples is based on a sacred union of love.

→ Prayer greatly strengthens the union of marriage.

→ Remember to pray for each other and for your children.

→ Discover what prayer projects God has in store for you and your spouse.

→ Ask God to heal the wounds between the two of you.

Chapter Ten: The Lord's Prayer (Our Father)

We're all familiar with this prayer that Jesus taught to his disciples. It appears in the Gospel of Matthew (Chapter 6) and the Gospel of Luke (Chapter 11). We can use the Lord's Prayer as the perfect pattern for complete prayer to our loving God.

This task is arduous. If you are going to pray this prayer in all its depth and breadth, you'll need a good hour at least to do so. This requires a certain level of experience, maturity and commitment. Anyone though can build up to these tasks. Construct your prayer life day by day.

Remember that prayer is a central part of our relationship with God. It is not a spare time endeavor but rather something that gives us life.

So we begin with:

Our Father, who art in heaven, hallowed be thy name.

Here you invoke the presence of our beloved Father in heaven. You praise him first. You recognize his holiness and his worthiness in all thanks and praise. You might pray, "Dear Lord, dear

Father in heaven. I worship you, I thank you. You are worthy of all praise. Blessed are you, oh Lord."

Continue praying in this manner. In awe and reverence, you invoke the presence of God and know that this time is for him and his purposes. Here you fill yourself with the fear of God, meaning the moment is of the utmost seriousness and deserves your deepest respect.

Thy Kingdom come,

God's Kingdom is his government. There is an order and there are leaders. And through our prayers, this Kingdom grows and becomes stronger. It can be an internal process as "the Kingdom of God is within you" (Luke 17:21). It is also an external, or global, process. However, in the end we must remember it all belongs to God.

For example, you can start by praying:

"Lord, establish your order in all things. Start here with me today. Establish your Kingdom in my heart, in my interior and in my life. Establish your order in my marriage, my family and in my home. Let your Kingdom come to me and my life, oh Lord. All power and authority are yours, oh Heavenly Father. Take control."

Then you might pray for the Lord's Kingdom to be established in each member of your family by name. This point is worth stressing. Focus first on your relationship with God then on your spouse (if you are married) and your children. Your home is the most important place where you serve God, and it should take its proper place in your prayer and in your life. You must ask for God's presence here above all else.

Later you can pray for your church, community and country. You should also pray for religious leaders as the pastors of the flock urgently need your prayer support.

You can also ask for God's Kingdom to be established throughout the world. You could pray:

"Dear Father. Establish your Kingdom in every continent, every nation, every city and every town. In palaces, in houses of government and in corners where misery and poverty abound. Amongst kings and presidents, and the poor and the wretched, Lord, may your Kingdom come."

Finally, pray that God permits you to be an instrument in spreading the Good News. Believe it or not, this might be the hardest part of being a Christian. It can be overwhelmingly difficult to share the news that Jesus came and died for our sins and that he will come again. You must pray for God's help here in order to be effective. Pray for this, then go out into the world and share the Good News. This is the most direct way for you to help build God's kingdom.

Thy will be done, on earth as it is in heaven,

This is a statement of acceptance – that things will be done God's way and by his timeline. It's also a prayer of faith that things will change. You pray that all things earthly will bow down to a heavenly order and power that is God's will. Again, as an example you could pray, "God, in all things, in my life, in my situation, let your will be done. Show me your will, oh Lord, that I might accept it and think and act accordingly. I trust in your will."

You could also pray, "Oh heavenly Father, that in the life of (person's name) your will be done, not mine." You could extend the same prayer to a group, situation or even an entire country. In many ways this part of the Lord's Prayer backs up or parallels the part of invoking God's Kingdom.

Give us this day our daily bread,

Here you can finally ask for something just for yourself. But how do you ask? In the perfection of this prayer, all that has gone before prepares how you ask. You don't ask selfishly but rather in terms of God's Kingdom and Will. So exactly what is the "daily bread"? It's God's Spirit and God's Word. It's Jesus Christ himself that you ask for.

You can pray, "Dear Father, give me my portion of bread for the day. Give me your Spirit. Give me your Holy Word. Give me the bread that is Jesus himself. Fill me and feed me. You are the source and sustenance of my well-being."

Now obviously, you can ask for your material needs as well, but as you immerse yourself in the pre-established concepts of Kingdom and Will, you will find your personal needs are quite small. You come to understand that if we seek his presence, God will satisfy all your needs, both spiritual and material.

And forgive us our trespasses,

At this point in the prayer, you ask for forgiveness – for your sin, action or any attitude that goes against God. Personally, I often find myself here asking God to forgive me for my pride, arrogance and vanity. Or for my lack of trust in him. Each one knows of what they must ask forgiveness, and our heavenly Father also reveals over time what you need to work on – or rather let him work on in you. Many times, you need to ask to be forgiven for failing to do right, or as some call it, the sin of omission.

I sometimes come to this point with no specific sin to confess. Still, I ask for forgiveness and continue to repent. Then, in a loving and character-building way, the Lord shows me things about myself that need attention. Nobody likes being told that they are sick. Nobody likes being shown that they are cowardly or immature. I certainly don't. But Jesus is the great physician, and only he can truly heal our deepest wounds.

As we forgive those that trespass against us.

Here you forgive others. Maybe you might think that you don't have much to say. Or maybe you have volumes to forgive. Either way the conviction usually makes a clear mark upon your heart. I often include here a prayer such as, "Lord, give me a merciful heart. Let my heart show the mercy that Christ shows towards me."

And lead us not into temptation,

In this part you ask for God's protection from your harmful desires. When you sin, you make a choice. Your transgressions require your participation. So at this point you ask God to protect

219

you and give you strength to avoid the lusts of the eyes, the flesh and the pride of life (1 John 2:15-17). You ask him to give you the strength, courage and discernment to avoid those situations, people and places (virtual and real) that can cause you to sin.

But deliver us from evil.

This is the final battle cry of our Lord. Jesus knew that there exists a great battle between good and evil. Our prayers are the ultimate weapon against evil. They are the ammunition that God uses against the enemy on all fronts. This is because it shows a complete trust and dependence upon him and his Holy Spirit to fight and win this Great War. And make no mistake, the victory has been decided. The cross on Calvary and the empty tomb are not only the evidence but the essence of our victorious God.

You might pray, "Dear Lord. All power, might and authority are yours. Push back into the abyss the forces of evil that try to invade my life and my family. Do not permit the enemy to influence my life in any way. In the name of Jesus Christ, I reject all attacks, deception, contamination, intrusion, traps or curses that come from the evil one. Any and all presence of evil I reject and return in the almighty name of Christ Jesus."

In this spiritual warfare you can pray for specific situations, people or communities in a similar way. Always remember that this prayer must be in the name of Jesus Christ.

After you finish the Lord´s Prayer

As we mentioned at the beginning of this chapter, this type of prayer can be exhausting. It is also incredibly revealing. As you go along, God will show you things and speak to you in miraculous ways. He will reveal things about his character and your character. He'll also show you areas where you lack strength or structure, and this is where he will build upon his grace. He'll lead you to passages in scripture that will give you clarification and confirmation. This process is serious spiritual exercise.

When you finish, you'll probably feel drained or empty. Or you might feel ecstasy. Either way it serves you well to fill yourself with the Holy Spirit. So before finishing, give God thanks and praise, and ask him to restore and fill you with his Spirit.

You can pray:

Fill me Lord. Restore me.

Fill me with your Holy Spirit.

Fill me with your loving restoration.

Fill me Lord with your Holy Spirit and love.

Amen.

Chapter Eleven: The Night Vigil

Before choosing his twelve apostles "Jesus went out to a mountainside to pray and spent the night praying to God" (Luke 6:12). Whenever you have to make a big decision, or need an important answer, the nighttime vigil is often required.

In many Christian traditions, these types of prayers are done in groups or in shifts. It may be a prayer for someone who is ill or even after someone has passed away. Oftentimes the night vigil is held before an important religious holiday. However, your personal vigil is different as it's just between you and God alone to address specific issues in your life.

I do offer one word of advice that accompanies all types of consultation prayer. Do not expect a definite answer just because you hold a prayer vigil. This is something that sometimes must be repeated. One personal example for me recently occurred when I was fasting and praying throughout the night looking for clarity on an important personal issue.

The night was filled with spiritual highs and lows, and even some periods of dozing off. I had put in the time and effort, but in the end, I felt frustrated as God had not revealed anything definitive to me. I eventually fell asleep around 3 a.m., and I had planned to end my fasting period with breakfast. However, in the busy morning hours of getting the kids off to school, I didn't have time to eat. And later that morning, God called me back to prayer and to searching his word. Only then did he deliver his message. Remember, it's always on his time and his terms. Be persistent and patient.

Now you might be thinking, "This is crazy. I'm not going to stay up all night praying when I could do the same thing during the day". While this may be true, think about this. How many times have you stayed up late watching a movie? Or attending a party? Or just talking with an old friend? When you understand God – in the form of the Father, the Son and the Holy Spirit – you understand that these are all persons, and then God becomes personal in your life. Sometimes the best way to get to know someone is pulling an all-nighter with them.

At night, all is still and everyone is asleep. You are pretty much guaranteed not to be disturbed by anything. In this silence you seek the Lord. Yes, you will get sleepy and may even fall asleep. But press on. Seek him with all your will and might. Let him know how important his response is to you. I'm not saying you have to stay up all night with no sleep at all, but make this time special. Again, that late night conversation with an old friend never ends in a 30-minute chat.

The sunrise prayer can be a component or variant of the vigil prayer. If you have the privilege to be on an east coast beach, this can be a special time between you and the Lord. Set your alarm clock for about 15-30 minutes before dawn and go out to a place where you can see the sun rise. Then just begin to pray and give praise to God. When the sun appears, you will see the glory of his creation. This can be one of the most powerful prayer experiences you can find. Always remember though, it's not the experience that should drive you, but rather your desire to honor and glorify Christ Jesus.

Sometimes you might be awakened in the middle of the night with an urgent feeling to commune with God, or maybe a sense of uneasiness will wake you. Don't ignore this call. Pray instead. Many times, the Lord awakens us from a slumber to reveal his will to us or to give us clarity about an important life situation.

The nighttime prayer is for answering big questions. Jesus used it to consult with God about who the twelve Apostles would be. This was perhaps the biggest decision of Jesus' ministry. So he went to seek his Father's presence alone. On the mountain side, Jesus spent the night in prayer. Follow our Lord's example when you have a big decision to make or major questions to ask.
****

KEY CONCEPTS: One of those days Jesus went out to a mountainside to pray, and spent the night praying to God. (Luke 6:12)

→ The night vigil is reserved for special circumstances.

→ It should reveal how much you value the Lord's presence and attention. Remember, it's about Him.

Chapter Twelve: Your Intimacy with the Lord

Sometimes you just need moments alone with God. No structure. No set method. You just need to be in his presence, the presence of perfect goodness. Maybe you need to heal or be restored. Maybe you are tired from the struggle. Don't let these moments go to waste. David expressed this much better than I can. In Psalm 63 David prayed:

O God, You are my God; I shall seek You earnestly; My soul thirsts for You, my flesh yearns for You, In a dry and weary land where there is no water.

Thus I have seen You in the sanctuary, To see Your power and Your glory.

Because Your lovingkindness is better than life, My lips will praise You.

So I will bless You as long as I live; I will lift up my hands in Your name.

My soul is satisfied as with marrow and fatness, And my mouth offers praises with joyful lips.

When I remember You on my bed,

I meditate on You in the night watches,

For You have been my help, And in the shadow of Your wings I sing for joy.

These kinds of words only come from a moment of deep intimacy with God. They may appear after a long moment of silence in his presence. Afterwards you might even discover responses to unasked questions that you had a profound longing to know the answer.

You will find yourself feeling and expressing a deep love for God and for His Son. It often becomes nearly unbearable, the strength of this love. From here you are fed and strengthened. From here your faith becomes as firm as steel as any doubt about the love of the Father is extinguished.

Sometimes you'll find yourself blessing and praying for others in these exchanges as love wants to expand and share. You'll find your prayer and intercession for others at these moments reaching a whole new level, especially for the person you struggle with or that frustrates you. Suddenly, mercy overflows for your enemies and nothing is more powerful in its healing nature.

These moments of deep intimacy with God can be exhilarating. Don't be afraid to enjoy these encounters. But remember, it is not about emotions. The Holy Spirit is the Spirit of truth.

It is about creating a hunger to come to know Jesus more. It is about the production of good fruit in all areas of your life. It is about the King taking control.

Conclusion: Be With Him, Be Like Him

Too many times we say that God is everything to us. If so, are you living a victorious life that goes along with this?

Why doesn't it show then? Why are our families in shambles? Why do we crumble in front of life's challenges? Why do we struggle with depression and anxiety? Why do we put more faith in pills and science instead of God? Where is the fruit that should be plainly evident if God is indeed at the center of our lives? Why do we dedicate so little time to him if he is everything?

Do you feel joy?

There are few guarantees in life. However, the worthiness of prayer is guaranteed. If God is the center of your life, then your time spent with Him should be at the center of your life. Then all your life's activity will radiate from this and be saturated with God's grace.

Faith breeds action. Prayer is an active process. If the time is invested, in a determined and intentional manner, then the fruit will come forth. And it will come forth abundantly.

If you want strength, they pray for it, and God will give you firm spiritual legs to stand upon.

If you want hope, then pray for it, and God will open the heavens to you.

If you want a merciful heart, then pray for it, and God will remove your heart of stone and give you a heart of flesh.

There are very few things in this world that can change your character. Your character is impregnated into your very being, where thought nearly disappears and almost instinctive behavior takes over. Good or bad, character is exceedingly difficult to change.

Prayer changes your character. It makes it godly. It makes it holy.

No, you will not become perfect or live a perfect life. On the contrary, you will find yourself in trials that are faced only by disciples of Jesus Christ.

Prayer will break you down, turn you around and spit you out again. It will reveal the innermost secrets about you. It can be arduous or even terrifying.

But in the end, it shapes your character in a godly way... and it lets you see yourself as you really are. Because you will see yourself as your Father in heaven sees you.

Fragile... weak... vulnerable... in total dependence upon him as your very life depends upon God's life-giving Spirit. You will see yourself as loved for who you are. You will see yourself loved desperately and unconditionally.

You will understand truth and freedom in their most complete forms.

You will come to know the Spirit that guides you.

You will fall in love with Christ.

You will be with Him and you will be like Him.

If you enjoyed this book, please leave a review for me. It means a lot to me!

About the Author:

My name is Vincent H. Chough, and I was born and raised in Pittsburgh, PA. In 2004, Jesus Christ changed my life. From there I began to leave behind all the horrible stuff that was damaging my soul.

In the past, I worked as a physician in the USA. I left that profession behind since God called me to a different task. Now I live in Argentina, South America, and I am grateful for all the blessings I have received here.

My wife and I are united in the heart of Christ. I serve my sons with a dedication that was impossible for me before. I am an imperfect man, but I cannot deny the work the Holy Spirit has accomplished in my life.

In November 2023 I was ordained as a Catholic deacon. A big part of my service includes coordinating a men's prison ministry here in Buenos Aires.

Only by doing my best to follow God's plan was I able to give up the things that poisoned me, my family, and the world around me. When I understood and embraced this fact, I was free to grow as a human being.

My writing doesn't mean that I've arrived at a destination. Instead, I share my experiences, both past and present. Hopefully my words will inspire others to continue along the way the Lord called us to travel. Millions of souls cry out for us to respond to his call.

May God's hand be upon you always.

www.ingramcontent.com/pod-product-compliance
Lightning Source LLC
Chambersburg PA
CBHW071957040426
42447CB00009B/1366